CHANTAL AKERMAN was born in Brussels on 6 June 1950 to Holocaust survivors from Poland. Her mother, Natalia (Nelly), was the only member of her family to survive Auschwitz. Akerman studied filmmaking in Brussels but, finding it too didactic, left after a term. She funded her first film, *Saute ma ville*, by trading diamond shares on the Antwerp stock exchange. It premiered on Belgian TV and Akerman couldn't afford to buy it back for many years. She spent time in Paris and Jerusalem before moving to New York in 1971, where she worked as a clerk, waitress, model and porn cinema cashier to finance *Hôtel Monterey* and *La Chambre*. These early films established her meticulous long-take style and her interest in contemporary urban life, particularly its ambiguous or transient spaces. She returned to Belgium in 1973 and produced *Je, tu, il, elle*, which the film theorist B. Ruby Rich described as the 'cinematic Rosetta Stone of female sexuality'. *Jeanne Dielman, 23 quai du Commerce, 1080 Bruxelles* premiered at Cannes in 1975 when Akerman was 25, bringing her to international attention. Over more than three hours, the film follows the daily activities of Jeanne Dielman, a widowed mother who cooks, cleans, looks after her son and engages in occasional sex work. Akerman called it 'a love letter to my mother'. This attention to the private and unrepresented details of women's lives – as well as the violence that lurks under the mundane – would engage Akerman across her filmmaking. She rejected straightforward narrative and conventional storytelling, focusing instead on things unsaid and unseen, but her output was wide-ranging, from adaptations of Proust and Conrad to experimental documentaries to rom-coms. The generational trauma of the Holocaust was an important preoccupation and led to her final film, *No Home*

Movie (2015), the filmic counterpart to My Mother Laughs, which features long conversations between Akerman and her mother, circling Natalia's illness and her wartime experiences. News from Home (1977) and Letters Home (1986), both epistolary movies, explore the relationship between mother and daughter through their correspondence. D'Est, her 1993 documentary on the collapse of the Soviet Union, was the first film she reconfigured as a video installation, breaking the singular projection into multiple channels. She went on to exhibit at galleries across the world and at the Venice Biennale and documenta. In 2011 she joined the faculty of the City College of New York as the first Michael and Irene Ross Visiting Professor of Film and Jewish Studies. Her other books include Une Famille à Bruxelles, which she performed as a monologue, and the play Hall de nuit. Akerman died by suicide on 5 October 2015, a year after Natalia's death. 'I don't feel I belong anywhere,' she wrote in 1977. 'On the contrary, I have the feeling that I am only attached to the land under my feet. And even there the ground is often a bit shaky.'

DANIELLA SHREIR is a translator, editor, graphic designer and programmer based in London. She wrote her undergraduate dissertation on Akerman's films and is the founder-editor of the feminist film journal Another Gaze, which publishes essays and reviews about women as filmmakers and spectators as well as hundreds of interviews with women filmmakers.

EILEEN MYLES came to New York from Boston in 1974 to be a poet, and subsequently a novelist and art journalist too. A Sagittarius, their twenty books include evolution (poems), Afterglow (a dog memoir), I Must Be Living Twice: New and Selected Poems and Chelsea Girls.

FRANCES MORGAN is a writer, researcher and film and music critic based in London.

My Mother Laughs

Chantal Akerman

translated by Daniella Shreir

INTRODUCTION

MY MOTHER LAUGHS is only an immersive experience. Just as Chantal Akerman refused (at least publicly) the labels 'lesbian' and 'feminist' in her life and her art opting instead for the more precise, vague, relational term 'daughter', we as readers are cast into this shifting space of a world that hovered within spitting distance of Chantal Akerman's mother's death and the tangible end of both of their lives intersecting.

My Mother Laughs was written in her mother's apartment in Brussels. Chantal sequestered herself there to work in a tiny room where her mother (Natalia) keeps coming to talk, for the two to plan meals. Natalia complains that Chantal tells her nothing about her life and reading this book we dwell in the condition of being told: as readers and listeners we have access to a voiceover that closely and yet inexactly overlaps with the experience of Akerman's last film *No Home Movie*.

We stand on that same balcony, we look down into the yard and we triangulate and even top her mother pretty much because we know more than she does about Chantal's life and nonetheless we are strangers, intruders on the ceremony of this relationship between mother and daughter, one only severable by death. This document as written is only stops and starts but such addicting ones, which lured me in so utterly because (beyond decades of wild admiration for Chantal Akerman's work and the complete

I

goodness of the text) I also had a mother who died recently. I'm in my sixties, I am and am not a lesbian and a feminist, my dad was in the American army in World War Two so I feel I have been given this book as some kind of therapy but I'm very confident other people will people will feel this way too. The magnificence of this memoir is that it singularly tracks the shadowy condition of being a female reared in one of the unutterable silences that followed World War Two and specifically if you were a European Jew this meant your parents survived that war but their siblings and possibly their parents did not (Natalia always refers to these lost people as 'the vanished' which locks them into so much speculative fiction of this century) and so you are briefly on an island with one of them, those lost but alive people who have been violently separated from their past AND refuse to talk about it and in that manner they pass the silence on, unadulterated, full of feeling. Thus a permanent infancy gets passed too from parent to child such that the parent's unwillingness to analyse their own devastating loss and pain casts a shadow on their offspring, as well as a frightening closeness around them, and this book speaks clearly from the pith of that shadowy island and the person who wrote it if they were not Chantal Akerman filmmaker would still be its deft recorder.

This strange country is made even stranger being told by a 'lesbian' who has not broken from this mother in the 'normal' way, from this compelling relation, by marrying and making family but instead merges with and records the relation, fitfully seeking to extract herself becoming more and more mired in the story as it reaches its close and in the wake of the mother's death dives into death after her, Orpheus-like.

So small wonder this singing daughter is horrified by

her nephew's wedding in Mexico that was the mother's final journey and therefore all must go along. (And all are invited except for Chantal's girlfriend.) Chantal is awed at the absolutist regime of family, the ritual of passing itself unto generations.

'And everything, absolutely everything was photographed,' she repeatedly marvelled at the proceedings. The greedy inventory of a wedding viewed through her outsider's eyes is a travesty: the massive numbers invited to eat and drink and dance and pray and bless the union is the quintessential nightmare of the unwilling non-conforming daughter. This is the non-celebration, the negation of her own life's role. It recapitulates Chantal's journey in life of not being 'normal' – one's hair being messy, the entire enterprise of being a knight errant exemplar who refuses to duplicate the spectacle of the mother's own much vaunted spectacle of being the beautiful woman, the tight, spiffy, eloquent female being, possessor of the bounty that quickens and inspires the rest, greases the ship of family and yet sitting there right there at the table is a stowaway, a bad passenger who is in here somehow, a joke – what gets enacted at this moment is probably the most unforgettable scene of this book when Natalia makes a joke about this daughter's outré-ness and the table laughs. Even Chantal pathetically laughs trying to join in and we get the full heft of the fact that in this dyad the mother, a former beauty to the extent that even her present dilapidated state merely signals dying, no indignity there but only further evidence of bravery, a triumph, but this daughter's a joke – the joker is dying and of course in the looming absence of the joker, the joke will die too.

I might think of this whole book as a sneeze. Or a black hole imploding. A cartoon deployment of feeling into temporary space with unclear boundaries that manages to hold the entire narrative, be it the relationship and the world, twinkling in a momentary gory splendour in which everything shows till it fades, midsummer dreamlike. The tale of their love is both romantic and tragic. But most valuably, it is untold.

One gasps to have it, here and now. After the wedding we go home, back to Brussels. We get domestic again.

When Chantal Akerman (her status as world-famous filmmaker being both beside the point and the only reason we have the story) is castigated for non-compliance what's revealed is an ever present historically unexpressed site of pain, abuse and torture (do I exaggerate?) that's good-naturedly dealt under the heading of 'family', the bantering and light-hearted bullying that exemplifies bonding, except that one family member (here the storyteller) is out not in and that is the fun.

All the refugees of the world and the criminalised queers, the banned trans persons of the world are the butt of this same joke. I'm in and you're out and you must die.

After this the entire oeuvre of Chantal Akerman begins to read for me like 'the other wedding', a meticulously hewn new formalism performed a capella as she bobs in and out of the viewable canon of the avant garde, disregarding the patriarchy and its rituals deliberately yet embedded in it. In *My Mother Laughs* she is clinging to the side of the ship as it's capsizing.

This is that log of the final voyage that we are permitted to read. How can this even be! The look of it on the page is just as enmeshed as their relationship. Chantal and her mother's lines merge, bump up, complete each other on the same line.

Sometimes you don't know who's talking and you know that is always the point. The strophes of this dialogue, this dispatch from a fading country, mother and daughter homeland are surging, rough and approximate.

It feels like poetry and it feels like action. One thinks screenplay too though no screenplay looks like this (but it feels like this). A passage that iterates quick exchanges between mother and daughter:

> She says, they've really conned me this time at the hospital. They told me it'd just be a small operation, nothing serious, but now I realise it's the opposite, that they'll be messing with my heart.
> Stop worrying about it.
> She sighs and says no.
> Then she groans without realising it.
> I leave the room.
> I come back in and ask her why she's groaning.
> Am I groaning. I'm not groaning.
> She can't hear her groans.

The text is free to move all over the page, like any hybrid work and because it does have a multitude of slight or exact echoes of films Chantal Akerman made and would make this book, again, is a shadow, an unmakeable thing that not so much tells all but defies the weightiness of the apparatus using film's function instead (or preceding it) and the economy of the page is flat but endlessly less encumbered than any work that's made holding a camera. This is an interior notebook of that. It is quick and silent, its purpose is sacred. In its stealth, in its forthcomingness, *My Mother Laughs* resembles a prayer.

Akerman gives us a word at one point, *sura* or *surah*. It's a term referring to a passage of the Qur'an. She sees one pinned to the wall in a New York deli. The Qur'an is composed of surahs, these surges, irregularly occurring. There's one that is three lines long and others that run for pages. (Akerman, a Jew who was bipolar, in her manic phases loved telling Arab cabdrivers about the resemblances between the bible and the Qur'an.) But the book is organised like that into sections like those recited by Muslims at different times of the day and are even tagged to locations (Mecca, Medina) where the revelations that spawned the text occurred. Of course that too has its resonance here considering the reterritorialising nature of this book (New York, London, Mexico, Brussels, apartments, planes, relationships) while the only real location is God/mother/home. The multitude of short and long passages of *My Mother Laughs* are the form of its composition and the sections mime the movements from room to room in the Brussels apartment, in the aggravating home of God, the only being in this universe which one may never transcend. Always to return to 'home', to palp the heartbeat of the endeavour from the originary location of a beating strophe between two women, that this wild, sentimental, ruthless text can only evoke.

EILEEN MYLES
New York, August 2019

I wrote it all down and now I don't like what I've written. That was before, before the broken shoulder, before the heart operation, before the pulmonary embolism, before my sister and my brother-in-law called me so I could say goodbye to her (for ever). Before she returned home to Brussels for the last time.

Before she laughed.

Before I realised that maybe I'd got it all the wrong way round.

Before I realised that my vision had been narrow and delusional. And that this was all I could manage. Not even faithful to my own truth.

For now, my mother is alive and well. That's what everyone says and everyone also says that she's strong and nobody understands how she's managed to survive.

She hurts all over but her hair has grown back. It's a miracle.

She's put on the weight she lost. She can just about manage with her broken shoulder. She needs help getting dressed and undressed, cutting up her meat and buttering her bread. She can't go for a walk on her own either and that's a real shame. Luckily she has Clara, who lives with her, in a room at the other end of her apartment. That way each of them has some privacy. Clara comes from Mexico. She's the sister of Patricia, who's her cleaner.

Every Christmas and every New Year's Eve they throw parties and invite my mother. My mother says that even though Christmas and New Year mean nothing to her she's happy to be invited and that Mexicans know how to create an atmosphere and she loves an atmosphere. She returns home from these parties pink-cheeked and bright-eyed.

Often she laughs in the middle of her moans. She still knows how to enjoy herself.

I listen to her laugh. She laughs over nothing. But this nothing means a lot. She even laughs in the morning sometimes.

She wakes up tired but she still gets out of bed ready to start her day.

I came home from New York to spend a few days with her.

And I don't know why or how but she's letting me be.

My mess doesn't seem to bother her anymore. She doesn't seem to notice it. She accepts it. She accepts me as I am. It wasn't like that before but since her brush with death, since she pulled through, she's changed. She knows what matters and what doesn't and she accepts me.

Sometimes she talks about when I was born and the fact that her milk didn't agree with me and how horrible it was to watch her child get weaker every day. One day she found a type of milk I liked. What would have happened if she hadn't.

Then she laughs.

I like the sound her laugh makes.

She sleeps a lot, but she laughs. She enjoys herself. Then she sleeps.

She's even come to accept her age. She knows she has to sleep in the middle of the bed so she doesn't fall out of it at night. She knows she should leave a light on in the corridor that leads to the bathroom. She knows there's someone at the other end of her apartment, not far from her, just in case. She knows all of this and she's OK with it. She likes it, even. She likes it when Clara comes out of her room. She likes to talk and laugh with her. They look like two friends who've known each other for ever.
  It was my sister's idea. She didn't think my mother could carry on living alone so Clara came back to Belgium from Mexico with her and for now it's working out.
  She likes Mexicans, by which she means Clara's sister and her sons who sometimes come over to say hello and eat with her. They're warm and laugh with her. It does her good. It does her so much good that she can't do without them. She's always liked having guests. Even the plumber who had to bring his daughter along with him. It was an emergency. I'd spent all night emptying buckets of water into the sink because there was a leak coming from the neighbours' upstairs and it wouldn't stop. It was a big event, and she couldn't help but enjoy it, even though she asked why it was happening, even though she said that her building was ageing badly and that she hoped that it wouldn't cost her a lot because she lives on very little and if she had to pay for repairs on top of everything else she didn't know what she'd do.

She knows she can count on her daughters but she doesn't like to. She doesn't like asking for things. She wants to make do with what she has which isn't much. She worked with my dad for most of her life but she wasn't on the books. So she has to make do with her German pension and the reparations she receives as a former prisoner of war. And with the apartment that my father bought me so that I could have something to call my own.

We sometimes rent it out for a bit of extra income but it doesn't bring in very much because the apartment isn't in great condition so we don't bother to rent it out that often.

When the plumber arrived with his little girl, my mother was so taken with her and her plaited hair that she became overwhelmed. It was beautiful to watch and the little girl was quiet and smiled. My mother gave her orange juice to drink.

The plumber had a special machine for unblocking the pipe and it made a terrible noise but it worked so I didn't have to spend the next night with the bucket.

The plumber told her that it could happen again because the pipes were so old. My mother said let's wait and see. One thing at a time. She said that if it happened again in ten years' time she might not even be around and my sister would have to deal with it because I'd never been a practical person. But I was the one who phoned the plumber and persuaded him to come, even though it was Christmas. She laughs.

She finds it hard to leave her apartment. She hardly ever goes out and that's all she talks about, but it's winter and it's dark and damp. And she knows that the damp is dangerous when she's been so ill. But even when it's a little less damp, which sometimes happens in Brussels in December, she doesn't go out. Only onto the balcony, that's it. She looks at the bleak garden belonging to the ground-floor neighbours, she looks at the cat, she looks at the dog.

She sees the bench, overturned by the wind which has taken everything along with it. But apart from that there's no one in the garden. The kids don't hang out there anymore. They're probably indoors. From spring onwards she'll see them and will enjoy seeing them. She waits for springtime and knows that it will come and that when it does she'll hear the birds flying overhead. She likes that.

But I can't stand it. I can't stand waiting for spring. I'm stuck in winter with its dark, heavy clouds that look like they'll stay for ever.

I feel like it's the end but it's not the end.

I don't know what I'll do or where I'll live or if I'll end up going somewhere else. But I know I'll leave for my apartment in Paris. I have an apartment. It's my home. That's what other people say, my home.

But I don't feel like I have a home or an elsewhere. There's nowhere I feel at home.

Sometimes I think I'll go to a hotel, a home away from home where I'll be able to write.

I read through everything I had written and I felt very disappointed. But what can I do. I wrote it. It's there.

Sometimes I tell myself that if I rework it then it might disappoint me less. But during the months when I was unable to do anything I kept telling myself that I'd start writing again soon, or that I'd continue what I'd started and that it would be good.

My mother is asleep in her reclining armchair, like the sort you get on planes. It's special, like the ones in business class. She loves this armchair and often falls asleep in it – that way she doesn't feel like she spends all day in bed.

It's terrible to be in bed. It's best not to be there, except at night.

During the day she sleeps in the living room in her armchair and still feels like she's alive. If someone rings the doorbell she can still hear it even though her hearing is bad, she goes and opens the door, smiling. She is so happy to have heard something and so happy that someone is there. Especially as it's Andrée and she loves Andrée. Andrée is a tall blonde woman who loves to talk. My mother loves to talk too so they get along well.

It's Friday and she is going to eat fish tonight and is excited.

Tonight we'll eat sole goujons. Sole goujons are little pieces of fried sole. She likes sole goujons. I like them too but I don't get excited at the prospect of eating them and I ask myself why not.

She gets excited, so excited that I end up getting excited too.

She says that the goujons taste much more delicate than normal sole.

Andrée comes to help her every Friday but she starts getting excited about it on Thursday. She thinks about the goujons and about Andrée, who has such good manners.

She loves Andrée, she loves the way Andrée cooks the goujons, in a sauce with parsley and butter.

She knows everything about Andrée, including the fact that she has two sons who are so well brought up as she puts it, that one of them is even training to be a lawyer. She knows that Andrée's husband is a superintendent in the department of civil law enforcement and that he never takes his weapons home with him. He doesn't want his two sons to get used to them. He doesn't want his two sons to work for the police, he who has seen too much. My mother understands that.

She understands everything, or nearly everything. And Andrée's life interests her. The lives of the people she meets interest her and as soon as they tell her something even slightly funny she laughs.

She laughs with Samira, with Maria, with Sonia, she laughs with all these women.

These women whom we call carers.

And my mother who can do next to nothing by herself anymore, and who certainly can't wash or get dressed or do lots of other things, has been given carers to help with the day-to-day. They shop for her and make her lunch and wash her.

She can still ease herself into the bath and she loves that. She holds onto the steel handrail and the carer checks whether the water is the right temperature and washes my mother gently and my mother is happy. She feels better for it.

My mother doesn't at all mind her carers seeing her naked. Luckily, she's never been embarrassed by things like that, including being seen naked. Anyway, she's had to get used to it. It was different for my father, who was a very discreet man, although when he fell seriously ill, he too had to adapt. My mother is a modern woman so nudity doesn't bother her. That's not to say she doesn't experience shame. But just the right amount, no more. So things like that, nudity especially, don't bother her. I wouldn't say I'm the opposite, but sometimes I do wonder. I'm my mother and my father combined: one minute I'm embarrassed and the next not at all.

One day there was no carer because it was Christmas Day, so I had to wash her myself.

She didn't mind being naked in front of me either, but I did. She liked me washing her, but I didn't.

I got on with it and that was that. I didn't tell her it embarrassed me and I told myself that I shouldn't be embarrassed. And anyway it didn't really bother me that much. No, not deep down. Just a bit.

Every day except Christmas Day the carer soaps her from head to toe, softly so that it doesn't hurt, and the smell of soap delights her. She breathes it in and says, that smells good. Then one carer or the other dries her carefully and takes her to her room to help her get dressed. Just her top half. She needs someone to help her get her pullover over her head and to slide the arm with the broken shoulder into one arm hole. She can almost always manage the second arm herself, but someone does it anyway. She can do the rest herself and is happy that she can.

Later she tries to use her right arm to raise up the left just like the physiotherapist showed her. She practises several times in a row. She asks me whether she's managed to raise her left arm higher than last time, she demonstrates, asks me yes or no and I say, yes, I think so. But I'm not so sure.

She's hopeful, she believes that she'll be able to do it one day, that she'll make progress, at least a bit of progress, enough to slice her bread, to dress and undress herself.

She thinks that at eighty-five she can still make progress, she really thinks so and she tries. And the physiotherapist congratulates her every time.

And he says, you're doing well. I don't know whether he really thinks so but that's what he says. He also says that my mother has a beautiful back and this makes her laugh with joy. He knows the compliments that work and he's quickly got the measure of my mother. And besides she's very flexible and by doing these exercises she's managed to strengthen her leg muscles.

She applies herself carefully to the prescribed exercises and the physiotherapist congratulates her.

When I'm there he says, would you take a look at that, those legs and that back.

He says that she's as flexible as a young woman. There are even exercises that he can no longer do because his body has become so stiff and he's only fifty.

He says that flexibility is something you're born with and that if you're not then you have to compensate by doing exercises and that as soon as you stop the flexibility disappears.

He shows my mother how stiff he is and tells her how lucky she is, she's always been flexible and that's what's kept her in shape and I'm the same.

And my mother laughs and after the physiotherapist is gone she repeats what he has said to her and she is very happy. She says, I've always been flexible and so have you. You must have inherited my flexibility. That's something at least.

What Clara who comes from Mexico likes, above all, is to

cook, and when there are a few of us at home she's happy and prepares more complicated dishes. Everyone congratulates her on her cooking and thinks that my mother is very lucky to have her around and it's true.

Unfortunately, she gets migraines, especially when I'm there, retinal migraines that can last for up to four days. Luckily I'm around to help my mother get dressed and undressed and to cut up her meat for her.

I think Clara chooses the weeks when I'm there to have these long migraines. She knows I'll do what needs to be done so all of a sudden the migraines come on.

My mother gets worried. Sometimes she knocks on Clara's door. She sees Clara with her back turned to her. When she can't see her face she closes the door and says, we should leave her to rest.

My mother respects Clara and her need for privacy. She wants nothing more than to go and see her but stops herself.

I tell her that when she feels better she'll get up, you shouldn't worry about her. She knows that we've tried everything to get rid of these migraines. In Mexico, my nephew took her to see a leading expert. He prescribed her some medicine but it didn't really do anything. This story makes my mother think of my nephew and she laughs. A joyful laugh. She loves my nephew.

A woman is lying in bed, moaning. It's a muted, repetitive moan.

She starts to say something, oh I don't know, I don't know. Does she know she's speaking aloud. She's deaf. She probably thinks she's only thinking it. She says aloud what she thinks without knowing that she's saying what she's thinking.

So we, her daughters, always know what she's thinking.

She's deaf but not entirely. There are things she can hear like the doorbell and sometimes even the phone but she doesn't like the phone because she has to guess what's being said to her. So my sister gave her a computer so she could use Skype because when she sees the mouth of the person she's talking to she's able to hear better. And she likes to see us, it makes her feel closer to us. She used to get very angry at computers and said she felt like she was from a different world and that the new world was rejecting her but with Skype she can manage.

So she spends hours and hours in front of the computer in case me or my sister log on and when we don't log on she gets annoyed but we can't spend all day logged on to Skype. Really we can't.

With Skype she can hear better because she can also see. But she still doesn't hear herself moan.

And when we ask her if she's worried she says no.

She says that she slept badly because she forgot to take her Bromazepam, she'd slept until 2 a.m., woken up, realised that she'd forgotten to take her Bromazepam.

So she'd taken one but hadn't got back to sleep.

Now she's in the kitchen eating her cornflakes.

She still has a few hairs on her head, she who was once so elegant. She who was once such a beauty. Everyone said so. And I was so proud of her, of my mother, this beautiful woman. And I loved her.

She's left the hospital. She knows that she almost didn't make it. She knows she's old but says she doesn't believe it. She wants to live.

She knows she'll have to go back for the heart operation.

She says that it's routine. She drags herself around the apartment while she waits. A real bag of bones.

She spends her time waiting for Patricia the cleaner to arrive. She likes her cleaner and the joy she brings. She likes it when she brings her sons with her and cooks for the four of them, she can hear them laughing. She likes that.

She's not sure if Patricia said she was coming today or tomorrow because the phone is always a bit of an ordeal, even with her hearing aid. She can hear something but she doesn't know what. Most often she guesses. Sometimes it's a good guess, sometimes it's a bad one. So she exists in a sort of limbo.

When she got out of hospital the cardiologist told her, take it slow before the operation. Of course she'll take it slow. How could she not. She drags herself around. Breathing has become difficult because of her aorta. She has aortic stenosis.

She can fall asleep at any time. Then she wakes up. Eats a bit. Exists.

She gets up, eats, has a bath. For the last few days she's managed to get in and out of the bath by herself.

She eats. Falls asleep on the sofa. Sleeps. Wakes up.

She talks a bit with her two daughters who are there for her. They talk about this and that.

Nothing serious.

What is there left to say.

Maybe after the operation.

She's a woman in a state of suspension. A woman who's survived. She knows it, that she survived and will survive again. Her time hasn't come yet, that's what she says.

I don't know if that's what she really thinks because

that's not what she says through her moans and her I-don't-knows that she doesn't realise are out loud.

I was there before she went into hospital and I was there when she came out again to prepare herself for going back in.
  She was very ill and I was scared, scared she would suddenly stop breathing in front of me, in her armchair.
  She fell asleep and I could feel the effort her heart was making to beat so I kept watch, breathe maman, don't leave me, breathe.
  Don't leave me, not yet. I'm not ready and maybe I never will be.

Breathing became so hard for her that we had to take her to A&E. In hospital they made her strong enough for the operation.
  They keep saying that the operation will be nothing. But will this bag of bones with its few hairs and dull eyes be able to hold out. One thing at a time.

I always say one thing at a time. I say one thing at a time knowing that anything could happen. But in this case there are only two things, life and death.
  And if life leaves her body, she'll leave with it.

MY MOTHER LAUGHS

CHANTAL AKERMAN

The child was born old and so the child never became an adult. They grew into the adult world as an old child and found it hard to adjust. The old child knew that if their mother ever died they'd have nowhere left to go.

As a teenager the child had lived recklessly, then as an adult they'd got by but only just, knowing they could always return home.

And since the death of their father, that had meant their mother's apartment.

As soon as the child got there, as worn down as ever by the adult life they weren't managing to live, they would go to sleep on the sofa for a few hours. Then, when they were a little less exhausted, they'd eat.

The child is her, it's me. And now I'm old, soon I'll be sixty. Or maybe older. And I'm stuck in this state. I don't have children. An old child doesn't have children. So what attachment will I have to this life after.

Can I live to sleep wake up eat go to bed. And listen to the radio. I had forgotten that. I often listen to the radio. I can't return to living recklessly. I'm happy to sleep as soon as the sun goes down.

Just four weeks until the operation.

That's what she said yesterday.

But after breakfast this morning she was tired out already. She went to sleep on the sofa.

When I went over to see her that's what she said, eating tired me out.

But am I allowed to rest? I told her that it wasn't about being allowed, that she had to.

Will I manage to stay here for four weeks.

I'll only manage it if I write. Anyway here or elsewhere, what difference does it make. I don't have a life. I never learned how to make one for myself. Here or elsewhere. But elsewhere is always better. So that leaving and leaving again and returning is all I've ever been able to do.

The first time I left I ended up in a tiny white room in Paris where it was cold.

Then somewhere else where it was hot. Then somewhere else again in a huge city on the other side of the Atlantic where I finally managed to feel well.

I felt well. I was finally living. I discovered new ways of life and other people even if I sometimes ended up walking through the city all night because I had nowhere to sleep. But most of the time I did. People invited me in and I could sleep and wash and even eat. I met up with some of those people again this year and they hadn't changed a bit. They were still just as welcoming. They still don't know how I ended up at their door. I don't know either. It's a mystery.

And in the hot place I very nearly ended up getting married because of the heat and because I didn't know what else to do and I felt worthless because I'd made a bad film so why not get married. At least then I could make someone happy, or my dad at the very least.

When I asked my dad why he was so keen on me getting married he said at least if I ever got ill I'd have someone to look after me. I often wonder how he knew that I'd get ill, very ill.

Maybe he just said it for something to say. He'd looked after his sisters when they were ill so he thought that all women got ill. Even though his mother was strong and only got ill after the war. During the war my father would leave the cellar where they were hiding, he'd go out to work, without wearing the yellow star. He knew it was better not to and all that time she stayed strong.

When the war was over things weren't the same. It's as if all her resources had been exhausted by it. Well, that's what I imagine happened. No one has said that. But it's either that or something else. I was told it was menopause or diabetes. But it was definitely something else.

My father never talked to me about his mother, but one of his sisters told me how much she loved her. She's the only one of the sisters to have married a non-Jew but she had her reasons. She loved him. She still does. And they look after each other. They are my youngest aunt and uncle. They have all sorts of illnesses but somehow they recover every time, probably because they look after each other.

My aunt loves her granddaughter. And her granddaughter loves her. She's also recently married and has a child. My mother showed me the photos. She married a Vietnamese man and you can see it a little in the child but everyone is very happy for her.

Luckily I'm not married because I would have been a widow a long time ago and when you're a widow it's for ever. That's what my mother who's a widow says anyway and one day she said, I should never have married someone older than me even though he was a good and honest man. Now I'm alone and it's for ever. I've always liked young people and I don't want to marry an old man again only to end up washing his socks. I'm just using that as an expression because now I have a washing machine. But I just can't imagine suddenly finding myself in bed next to another old man, a man I haven't even got old with. I'd just like a friend. Someone I could go out with, who would accompany me to the theatre, maybe even someone to go dancing with. Young people like to dance but so do I. At weddings and everywhere else, I love to dance and when I dance I feel I'm my true self. Especially if I dance for hours. That does me good. You know, I would have really liked to be a dancer or a singer or even a swimmer, maybe even a musician but I did nothing with any of those things.

That's why I'm so happy my granddaughter went to university. I'd like to see her do something with her life. I hope she doesn't become a widow. I know she's still young but you never know.

You never know what might happen and I know that better than most because what happened to me happened to me and who would have thought up such a thing. Well, someone must have thought up such a thing or it wouldn't have happened and besides it was so well organised. It'd all been thought through and considered. That's why I sometimes say that thought isn't always the best solution, even if it is final.

My eldest daughter always asks me to talk about it but I don't want to. I know that if I do I'll be lost. That's what I think anyway. My eldest daughter says the opposite will happen. That it's good to talk. But she doesn't talk about much either, I mean, she doesn't talk much about her life. Maybe she thinks that what she has to say can't be said to a mother like hers.

Sometimes I think that it's because of what happened to me. And sometimes I think it's the opposite. I don't know what to think so I try not to think about it.

And anyway it's possible that what happened could happen again.

There's no such thing as an end. It's possible that anything could happen again. Not in exactly the same way of course but a version of the same thing could happen, especially now there are all these people sleeping on the street, I see more and more of them every time I go out and I always have to turn my head away because I don't want to have to deal with it and because I have a big apartment and still I don't ask if they want to come and stay. Sometimes I think that would be a good solution but there's too many of them and there's more and more each day. And they're dirty. I know they can't help it of course but I can't stand the sight of dirt so that's one of the reasons I can't have them in my home. I do realise that after a warm bath and a good bowl of soup and with some new clothes they'd be clean again and that they weren't born dirty.

But I can't deal with this kind of dirtiness. I experienced it once and since then I haven't wanted to hear about it. And I especially don't want to see it, not in my home or anywhere else for that matter. It makes my heart sink and when I see it in the street I look away without even thinking and when I visit some areas like the area my daughter lives in in Paris and I see all these dirty mattresses in the street my heart sinks too and I ask my daughter how she's able to live with it. She says that she can't stand it either and that she tries not to see it especially when it's grey and raining. When it's sunny it's a bit better because

the mattresses look brighter so the stains show up less. I suppose it's true that you can see them a bit less but you can also smell them. Seeing isn't the only sense after all. And sometimes smelling is the worst of all of them. Except with flowers. But even then you can end up leaving flowers in water too long when you forget to change it and even when you forget you have flowers. You leave them for a bit and they start to smell funny. So you throw them in the bin without thinking. Or with meat. Sometimes the smell of meat is disgusting. And you mustn't eat it when it smells like that, even if you're very hungry. No, you really must stop yourself from eating it then even if you're woefully hungry.

She rarely gets hungry these days but she knows she must eat to regain the weight she lost and to stay well, so we spend hours discussing what might give her back her appetite and we always come to the same conclusion, she'll eat herring with onions any day of the week, either herring in oil or herring in brine it doesn't matter as long as it contains herring. She also likes shrimps but only in a salad with fresh onions and in a light mayonnaise dressing and the mayonnaise has to be well seasoned with salt and pepper or else she loses her appetite. And then there's the fromage blanc. She doesn't know what she'd do without fromage blanc and it's always at the top of her shopping list.

I like fromage blanc too but having spent so much time talking about it I can't bring myself to eat it. The thing I like most and the only time of day when I feel as though I'm really living is when I rush to the shop to buy cigarettes. All of a sudden I'm a person. A free person, a person with something to do. And today in particular because it's sunny after so many grey days.

I like to write down what's happened. Because then I feel as though I'm a person who has something to do even when nothing is happening.

But something always happens, small insignificant events.

The phone rings. Words are spoken and exchanged. Silence. Occasional sighs. The neighbours make noise. The lift sometimes gets stuck. The bins have to be taken downstairs and this often involves some words spoken and barely exchanged.

MY MOTHER LAUGHS

For now my sister is here. I haven't seen her for a long time and she's about to leave again. My sister has a life. And she knows about its pleasures. I watch her and wonder how she learned them.

She's known about life's pleasures from the moment she was born. And she has soft brown eyes. Her skin's soft too. She's a curvaceous and smiling woman.

Except sometimes when she gets angry. But her anger passes straight away. She gets angry as soon as something angers her. She doesn't wait for years like I do. I wait years before saying that something has made me angry, even when it's caused me to suffer terribly. And even then I need something else to bring the anger to the surface. Something that has nothing to do with the cause of my anger. Then I get angry. When I get angry I feel like my anger is horrible and that my cries and shouts will cause the world to shatter around me. That someone will die because of my anger. My anger is huge when I get going. And because it's usually me who gets hurt in the end I've come to resent it.

And when I ask L., did you see how angry I got, how

loudly I screamed, she laughs at me. You call that shouting? Yes. Then L. laughs even louder and I like to see her laugh. She has this crazy sense of humour, except sometimes when I try to make her laugh. Often when I try to make her laugh it falls flat. Sometimes she even gets angry and I can understand why. I hate making her angry and I end up not knowing what to do with myself so I do nothing in case it makes matters worse. I've only shouted at L. twice but both times I was under the influence. I didn't realise it at the time but I was under the influence when I thought I was just managing to let myself go. But you never really let yourself go when you're drunk, you only think that's what you're doing and for several minutes, several hours, several days even, you walk around with a strange sense of freedom. And as soon as that wears off you start asking yourself questions and you wonder whether you really needed to break someone's heart in order to enjoy a few seconds of freedom, a few seconds of what I now call false freedom.

When it's about something that doesn't really matter I can sometimes manage to shout even though deep down I know it doesn't really matter, and I'm very proud of having shouted. But when it's about something that matters the anger stays bottled up inside me and I get so tired out by it that I lie in bed sometimes for several days wondering why I'm so tired, so then I start to take vitamins. I tell myself that it must be my anaemia. During these periods I've even gone to see the doctor who has sent me for blood test after blood test, there's always something wrong with my blood but I'm used to it. I ask him if I shouldn't just get a full blood transfusion. He says no. Sometimes he says, let me have a think, well, we don't normally prescribe full blood transfusions and even if we did you know in the end your blood would come back into circulation, and suddenly I feel relieved. Deep down I wouldn't really like to have someone else's blood.

I don't know why I care so much about my blood. It comes from a dark place that I don't want to uncover. I know that if I did it'd reveal something to me about myself that I wouldn't like, so I prefer to leave it in the dark. Often it's better to keep things in the dark. Sometimes I'm struck by an urge to seek out a truth, but which. That's very important. You can sense in books or films when there's a truth. Even when it's hard to see, especially when it's hard to see. When there's a truth that's hard to see even when you know it's there something happens underground, slowly, sometimes very slowly, and suddenly, when you're no longer even thinking about it this truth comes to light and it's an incredible moment that doesn't happen every day and it's good, it's so good that you're struck suddenly by a feeling of weightlessness and calm.

Tomorrow my sister will leave. I'm already scared of her leaving. I'll find myself alone with my mother who has got into the habit of grabbing my face and kissing it with such intensity that I have to turn away. She speaks with such an overt sentimentality that me and my sister have to stop her. We stop her just in time.

So she says, I'm not even allowed to speak in my own home. But it's just that these aren't the words we want to hear. I don't know why. And when we laugh she says go on, go on, make fun of me. But we need to laugh. And sometimes we need to laugh hysterically. Because this blanket sentimentality threatens to overwhelm us and we don't know what to do with it, it's too heavy.

Sometimes we can feel its weight for hours. And neither of us likes it. It's too much. But my mother loves it. It's as though she believes it reveals our love for each other.

The love which is maybe already there, I don't know. Probably. A certain kind of love. I don't know.

Sometimes I think I should give my mother a dog. But she doesn't want one because of the rain and because it might make her fall over.

I found myself a small room in my mother's big apartment where I could write with the door closed. The bedroom is full of rubbish. But I don't really mind. I like it.

I have a refuge where I can write and smoke with the window open.

My sister said that she mustn't smell the smoke because it will tempt her and with my mother's weak heart it would be the end.

Today my sister drove her to the hairdresser. It was her first outing after leaving hospital, her first outing was to the hairdresser.

She said she could no longer bear to see herself looking so shabby.

Yes, just a few hairs left standing on the head of this woman who was once so beautiful. She finds it hard not to be so beautiful anymore. I can understand that. I can understand almost everything even though sometimes I don't want to.

That's why I always feel sick to my stomach.

And then it's back to the kitchen table.

It's lunchtime.

And even before she sits down to eat she asks loudly, and what will we eat tomorrow. What she means is when my sister is gone. But that's not what she says.

She wants to believe that I won't know how to cook for her.

I tell her that of course I know how, so she says that usually when I come to stay it's her who ends up cooking and then she tries to kiss me again and I wriggle out from her embrace and straight away I feel cruel and even stupid. What would it cost me, I could just let myself be kissed, she'd be so pleased.

But it's hard to see why I've remained an old child in black and white like that.

The reason I never knew how to make a life for myself.

The only thing that can save me is writing. And even then.

And even when I write it's about her and so it doesn't give me the sort of release that people who don't write might imagine. No, it's not a release. Not a real one.

At the table her eyes start to close.

Yes, the hairdresser tired her out.

Straight after eating she went to bed on the sofa. Now she's asleep.

I feel depressed. But it'll pass. Tomorrow. And even if I still feel depressed I won't reply to C.'s emails. That makes me feel strong. And I tell myself nothing can be done. But when there are no emails I spend my time waiting for them and I don't think about what C. must feel when she's in the same position, I think only of myself and how strong I am for being able to resist.

Now, after rereading all the emails she sent me over that period and all the others too, I regret it. Not our break-up, no. But the fact that I didn't say what I really felt.

All I feel is regret and I'd like to tell her so. But I know it's too late and that it's probably better for me to leave it unsaid and that this time I should bear her feelings in mind, not just mine.

All I feel is regret but only about the emails, not the rest.

That was the first time we broke up and I should have held out.

I held out for a little while but then she knocked on my door and I hadn't expected her so I couldn't bring myself to tell her go away. I just said, what are you doing here. I wasn't happy. But she acted like nothing was the matter and came in.

I should never have opened the door.

My mother appears at the door to the small bedroom.

Won't you talk to me for a minute, please. Am I annoying you?

No, it's not that, I just have things on my mind.

Well, you should work those things out.

Yes, I'll work them out.

Then I go to bed.

I hide in one room or another, then I feel ashamed for having hidden.

I return to the room where she sits. I try to think of something to say. Have you finished your book, I ask.

No, I can't, my eyes hurt. The words are all blurry.

I should never have asked her if she'd finished her book. I should have known I'd get an answer like that.

I stay there for a moment and then I go and hide again. But even when I'm hidden I can feel her presence, so I tell myself there's no point hiding. I might as well return to the room where she spends all day asleep, or half asleep. But just thinking about it makes my heart sink.

My heart sinks and a few tears follow. I wipe them away.

I return to her room as if to a funeral.

And then the shame comes back.

She tries to let herself get swept up by her mother's impeccable organisation. After two or three days she realises it does her good.

There's always something to eat in the fridge. They eat in a clean kitchen at the same times every day.

Not like in her apartment where there's never anything in the fridge except when she suddenly decides she should get her life together. But that's rare and even when she sets her mind to it she doesn't always manage the necessary steps.

Going downstairs and walking to the supermarket feel like insurmountable tasks, and so does returning a phone call or spending the evening with friends.

Often she will have arranged to go out but when it gets to the afternoon she says, I won't go. I can't go. I wasn't that invested in going anyway. She ends up phoning the person and making something up and saying, but let's do something next week, without being sure that she'll manage that either.

Sometimes it seems easy and she goes, especially if someone comes to pick her up.

But most of the time she stays in bed, takes sleeping pills and goes to sleep.

That's probably why her friend who's from New York, her best friend in New York and maybe even in the world, said to her when she told him that she'd met someone,

that's brilliant, you're going to have a new life, you can start over. But she's so young. That doesn't matter. I'd just met her and I didn't dare tell him how. I was embarrassed. I just said, she's beautiful and wonderful and intelligent, so my friend said, come out with us and bring her with you. Yes, I said, I'll come and bring her with me.

She looks like a wrinkled old prune or a newborn lamb, I can't decide which.

Do you love her? Yes, I think so. Yes, I think I love her. Maybe. I don't know.

She listens to me.

I talk to her all the time.

I shouldn't have.

It started at a conference on the speed of light and Hiroshima. The physics professor from the University of Nice explained that the dead bodies had left a lasting shadow and were built into the city walls.

And suddenly I realised that I should be trying to recreate something like that in my work with images. Yes, that's what I should be doing.

Then my sister came to meet me from Mexico and persuaded me to get a Facebook account.

And that's how it started.

I saw that people were discussing shadows so I joined in.

When the important professor left the room I'd wanted to talk to him. But he didn't seem like someone you could just approach. Maybe if he hadn't seemed like someone you couldn't just approach it never would have happened. Maybe. I don't know. Or maybe that was the pretext I used to talk to someone I didn't know. But I don't think so. The conversation was interesting so the next day I continued it. Yes, on Facebook. I tried to find it again but Facebook has made a fool of me. It says this conversation no longer exists and my memory is too short to remember it.

But anyway, after a short time the conversation completely changed. It was no longer about shadows, shadows had been replaced with more and more lots of love and speak to you soons. What else. That's it for the moment. For the moment yes but everything can change in an instant and so I would write shaking all over, waiting for her to wake up. I would stay in front of the computer and suddenly I would see a green dot appear to the left of her name and it would start all over again. It was exciting and emotional and it happened so quickly. And it went quicker and quicker. And I was happy.

So happy, I couldn't believe it. It could have continued that way, with us writing to each other. It could have and I would probably have been happy for the rest of my life, but one day we talked about our desire to see each other. And it could have remained a desire that we could have written about, with us saying how much we wanted to see each other and why. I was so happy and it was probably enough for me but I felt in my body and everywhere else this desire to see her and she felt the same. We were already telling each other how we'd kiss and how we could already feel those kisses, and that could have been enough. I was starting to live again. I would wake up excited, full up with what we'd said to each other the night before. I would go to bed reading the poems she'd sent me, after sending her anecdotes and songs, and I remember thinking that sending poems and songs is something you do at 15 but still I would listen to the songs on repeat and sing along, especially to 'My Funny Valentine' and 'Bang Bang'. These were the sad songs I would sing along to at the top of my voice.

I sang these songs over and over and it could have been enough, now that my heart was beating fast and my body had come back to life. I was so happy. I wondered if I'd ever been so happy in my life and more and more often one or other of us would say, I really, really, really want to see you.

Then one day it happened.

She wrote, I'm going to see if I can free myself up for two days next week to come and see you. I think it would be the best thing for both of us. Don't chat with any of your new FB friends or I'll get jealous. No I'm just saying that to wind you up.

Lots of love.

I should have seen the signs but I thought it was just her sense of humour so I laughed. If only I'd known.

At the last minute she couldn't come, she wasn't feeling well. And I felt a vague sense of relief. She had an abscess that was causing her discomfort. She often got abscesses.

I felt a vague sense of relief without knowing why, but probably because I already knew.

After that she said, you come instead. I said yes and then I said no. I'm not well. You won't like me when I'm not well. She said that she would, that she was good at dealing with things including my not being well, she could cope with that and with lots of other things too. I should have known that when someone puts your mind at rest so easily they're not always telling the truth, as they won't about lots of other things too.

Then someone else told me you should go, what's the worst that could happen. So I went to England. That was where she lived. In London's Zone 2. An area where everything looked the same.

I shouldn't have.

Today my mother woke up sobbing. Sobbing so hard it was heart-wrenching. Shouting, almost. I thought, this must be what horses sound like when they neigh. Even though I don't know horses very well. I don't know nature very well in general. I do know that being in nature is meant to be good for your breathing and I've often thought, I should go. But I've never known where in nature to go.

I knew that this sobbing was my fault. Even though I have always felt everything to be my fault even when it isn't. But this time it was. I couldn't stand being there and she could feel it, she knew I was hiding and running away from her.

So I made an effort to be kind and tender and it almost calmed her down.

I walked around the block with her, holding her firmly by the arm.

Her legs were shaky so we went very slowly. It was the first sunny day of the season and she hadn't been out for

seven weeks.

After a few steps we sat down outside a café in the sun. It was at a busy junction where cars passed by. She turned her face to the sun and closed her eyes. She looked beautiful, she looked happy.

It's good to be out, she said, it's nice. I really needed some sun.

Yes, I said, it's good to be out.

The sun was strong and I was starting to sweat and to feel annoyed by the traffic and the dust. But she wasn't sweating, she was soaking up the sun.

She kept turning her face to the sun and closing her eyes. She was half smiling with a look of terrible concentration. It was because of the sun.

She was wearing sunglasses because the optician had prescribed them for her dry eyes and she always did what the doctors said. But I could still see that her eyes were closed and that her head was turned up towards the Brussels sun.

I said, let's go. She said, five more minutes.

I didn't reply, I waited. I waited for the time to pass.

Finally we got up and returned home, her legs were still shaky and I was still sweaty.

She said, you keep running away from me.
She's speaking at last, I thought. She's finally saying something and it's the truth.
I was happy.
She wasn't saying I love you.
I could breathe.

I went to see her in hospital after she'd fallen out of bed in the middle of the night, it was the year after the heart operation which had ended up going well in spite of everything, even if it'd been a horrible experience. But after the operation, I don't know when, it's all a blur, she'd fallen out of her bed at night and had had to return to hospital and it was there that she said to me with such hatred that I thought I might faint, I can't stand to see you in that dirty shirt, that's what she said, you deserve a smack. She brought her hand up to her face like she was really going to do it.

I thought to myself, she must have been bottling up this hatred for years. That it was the reason for all the kisses she'd given and taken away. That I embarrassed her. My old clothes and unbrushed hair had always bothered her, hurt her even. It was the opposite of reassurance. An unwrinkled world. A very peaceful life without unironed shirts and nasty surprises.

She'd wanted to smack me and she'd said so. I felt happy without knowing why but I knew that something real had happened. I'd felt like I might faint but I was happy.
It was a good thing, I could feel it. I smiled. Not when she said it but afterwards. I bothered her and at least she

had admitted it for once.

The articles about me and my films made up for it a bit, but not entirely. She cut them out from newspapers to keep. But if I brushed my hair it would be better, much better.

I can't bear to see you in these shoes anymore, she said whenever I arrived at her apartment in old shoes.

Or in that jacket.

And at the restaurant when I dipped my finger in the sauce I thought she was going to explode.

I said, leave me alone. No, I won't leave you alone.

I'd really wanted to dip my finger in the sauce. And it was her local restaurant, the one on the corner, where she'd always see people she knew and kiss them on the cheek.

Then, she told me about them. Well not really about them, but about the fact they liked her, and that they'd known her as a young woman, when she was so beautiful.

These people were old like her. Old, well put-together Jews who were in better health than she was.

They weren't survivors. Nearly all of the women still had thick hair and better hearing than my mother.

All of these people gave her advice. They knew better than her and most of them had doctor sons whose advice they'd pass on.

These people were in the know. They knew about the heart, about insulin and dialysis. And they loved to talk about it. Sometimes they'd talk about other things but it was rare. They always ended up saying, with the authority of a doctor, when you have a weak heart you don't just jump on a plane to Mexico to see your children and grandchildren.

But the cardiologist hadn't actually said she couldn't.

Well she hadn't understood everything he'd said. But

he'd definitely told her that a narrow valve was common at her age.

Anyway it was on the plane that she had her first heart attack. This heart attack had saved her life. On the plane there was a young doctor who said straight away, she's going to need an operation. And that was what saved her life. My sister even had to board the plane when they landed.

A few days later we took her to the hospital in Brussels where she had the operation that saved her life. Without it her aortic valve might have slowly continued to narrow without her ever realising and it would have become inoperable and that would have been the end. So she'd been lucky, very lucky, but it wasn't over yet. One day, when everyone thought things had finally got back to normal, and when I was staying with her in the next room with the door closed, I heard what I thought was thunder or an explosion.

I got out of bed and found her on her back on the floor where she'd fallen. Her body was spread out on the carpet next to her bed. She'd probably been trying to go to the bathroom and some part of her body had given way so she'd fallen. I was horrified. Are you hurt? She wasn't sure. Come on, let's get you back into bed. In bed she still couldn't feel anything. Maybe it really was nothing.

I tucked her in. I asked her again whether she was hurt. No, she said, not at all. I went back to bed. Worried but not very. But I still felt horrified. I said to myself that this time she'd had a lucky escape but it could happen again and much worse. She'd banged her head and if she banged it again harder what might happen. My heart was beating fast and took a long time to calm down.

An hour later she was screaming in pain so I took her back to hospital. That was the day she lost the use of her left shoulder.

That was the week she threatened to smack me.

I loved her so much when she was young, my mother.

Her youth, her beauty, her dresses. Especially this one summer dress with thick golden and orange stripes. She looked so radiant in it. She would call me to help her do it up at the back and I loved that. Then she would ask me if she looked OK. Yes, you look beautiful. This dress really suits you. It brings out the darkness of your eyes.

And I would talk to her, tell her rubbish anecdotes.

Sometimes I would run away, especially when we were by the sea. But I was always found. Someone would always find me.

I loved her. But I still had difficulty eating. I still got dirty all the time. And I'd still go off and spend hours walking along the beach.

She also had a blue and white gingham swimsuit. Sitting in the sand we'd have discussions. I wanted a brother. You'll have one, or a sister.

I ended up with a sister and I never regretted it. But at the beginning I was a bit disappointed. A little bit. I loved her as soon as I saw her. She really looked like a prune.

Now she lives in Mexico and we Skype often. She doesn't like C. She says, she's not making you happy.

Even though C. would like me to be happy with her.

C. likes seeing me laugh, likes seeing me enjoy life with her.

But the opposite is what happened. The opposite.
Unhappiness.
But that was in New York. Before, when we didn't see

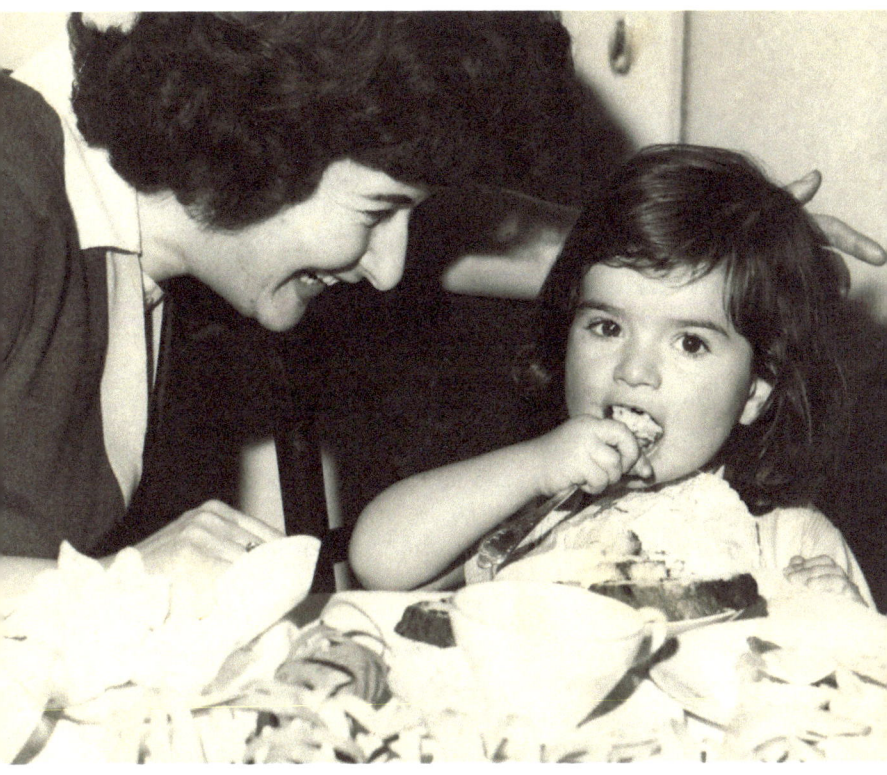

each other often, unhappiness hadn't had the time to settle in. But in New York it did.

She liked seeing me laugh but the opposite is what I gave her. I no longer laughed, I cried. I no longer spoke. Instead, a heavy silence. I was no longer floating. I'd left my body behind and with it hers.

How had I not understood?

We would watch TV and films, the films that we'd ordered on the TV. When we watched films we managed to live. Films were what we needed to live. Not in the same way as we'd lived at the start, but it was living all the same. Sometimes they allowed us to touch each other. Even to love each other a bit. Love each other at all. And sometimes to sleep. But rarely. Insomnia had swallowed us whole. Instead fatigue and tears. Then faint and subdued smiles.

One day she'd said to me, I can remember your smile when I opened the door to you in London. I spent a beautiful day with your smile. But if that's true then why did you tell me you had to stop yourself from throwing up when I said jokingly, I've got nothing more than half a dog to my name. At the time I couldn't understand it. I couldn't understand it but I started to question everything. I was the one who let the silence in. It was only after that I understood. If I only had half a dog to my name that meant that the other half still belonged to my ex-girlfriend. Which would mean that I wasn't over her like I'd said I was when she'd asked me.

Over-sensitive, proud, arrogant, shy, uncompromising, too much to handle, I'd ended up scratching at old wounds. I composed myself and said, I don't love you. I don't love you anymore.

That's impossible.

No. Yes. No. Yes.

I've made a home for you, she said to me one day. It was true, and I hadn't even noticed.

Yes, all the delivery men that had rung at the door one after the other were delivering things to make me a home but when I heard the doorbell I'd just say, not again.

She was bleeding and I hadn't even noticed. I hadn't seen a thing. Not even that her beautiful face had become dark and tragic. Not even that her pupils were disappearing. I couldn't see anything anymore. I couldn't even turn to look at her. Not even that.

She began to dissect every one of my gestures. She began to study everything I said, every phone call I made.

She said, do you think I don't know that you phone your girlfriends in Paris and God knows where when you go outside.

I said it's true but if I'm on the phone in the same room as you and I say lots of love back you go mad. I can't stand it.

It was only when we were in front of images that we could be in each other's arms and afterwards sometimes we would talk into the early hours.

Then we'd drink coffee until my stomach started to fight back.

So she'd bring me a camomile tea with the sugar cubes that had arrived with one of the delivery men.

After she was released from hospital my mother talked about nothing but doctors, her pain, and who would pick her up to take her to the airport.

And who would do her packing.

This time she really couldn't do anything anymore. Her hands were misshapen with arthritis and her feet were starting to look the same.

There was a new pain in her thigh.

Her eyes watered too much or not enough due to dryness.

And every day her thigh had to be injected to help strengthen her bones.

Without it she'd be full of sand. No longer an upright person but a bag of sand asleep in a bed.

But she was going to pull through. She knew it and so did I.

She started to come out with things like, no I can't for the life of me remember Polish anymore. Without anyone having asked. It had simply gone through her head so she said it aloud.

Why, I don't know.

But sometimes people would ask. Sometimes it'd occur to people so they'd ask. Sometimes it was the carers who knew she came from Poland and sometimes it was other people who had been told once and hadn't forgotten.

But none of the rest of her family who'd arrived with her from Poland was still around. Everyone had died from one thing or another, so she had no one to speak Polish to. So she didn't remember it anymore. Not well, in any case. Apart from a few words, at least that's what she'd say. I knew that she could remember more than that but for one reason or another she would say, I don't remember it.

As for me, as soon as I meet a Polish person I get out my three words of Polish and the Poles seem pleased but the conversation ends there. With three words you can't get much further than that and as soon as I meet someone Russian I get out my ten words of Russian and I'm happy and proud as if I were the only person in the world to know these ten words of Russian and the Russians reply as if I knew at least a hundred and I look at them and start to nod. But this makes it look as though I've understood something so the Russian person starts to speak more quickly and I get into a panic. Ya nie ponimayou, ya ne razumié, sorry I don't understand. I forget which language to speak, Polish or Russian, and when I'm in the street and I hear someone speaking Hebrew it's even worse. I say shalom ma nishmah, hello how are you, they reply, well, and walk past without even looking up and I feel hurt. I would like to connect with them and tell them that I learnt Hebrew when I was a little girl at the École Maïmonide and that it's my father's fault if I can't speak it better.

It's always someone's fault and my father had plenty of them even if I now think of him as a saint.

I know he's not really but actually he wasn't bad, though it took me years to realise it. Before that everyone would tell me what a good man my father was and I would refuse to accept it. For the most part, anyway. But later, I did. First I had to fall ill. When I'm ill I can speak any language, especially the ones I've forgotten like Hebrew. It suddenly comes back to me and I can read it as if I'd never forgotten it. Any excuse and I start mumbling in Hebrew. Even when it's not necessary.

And when I get in a taxi and the taxi driver is Arab I automatically try to convince him that Arabic has the same roots as Hebrew and I announce proudly that the word for one is echad in Hebrew and wahid in Arabic. The taxi driver isn't always convinced, but sometimes he is. And then I don't know why but I feel very happy and start to tap my feet in the back of the taxi and look out at the landscape, the Parisian landscape, and see how beautiful it is. Especially when there's a lot of traffic because then I have the time to look at it properly even though sometimes I'm worried about being late. When I'm like this I always think there's too much traffic even when there's hardly any at all and I have to remember to breathe through my frustration. But sometimes even when I remember to breathe my frustration still grows so I tell the taxi driver, just drop me here.

Deep down, I know that my father loved me, even though he once told his sister in Canada that his daughter was an odd one, not like the rest. I didn't know that he knew. I thought I'd managed to hide it from him but he'd understood. It had made him unhappy. That's probably why he was always silent around me and me around him. A loaded silence, as they say, but one that was full of undertones and in the end those undertones had become overtones so I was an odd one.

Anyway it was his fault too if you can talk about fault and even if you can't. Imagine wanting a boy instead of me. But it also suited me to think it might be his fault because it was also the fault of my mother and the rest of the world too. One day I said to my uncle, maybe if my mother hadn't always stroked me and held me tight against her body things might have turned out differently. But maybe not and anyway that doesn't matter, not really. Especially not now. But even so, let's just say that too much love is bad for a child. But you never know how much is too much and even when you do you say well it's not that much, there are worse things than that.

I never thought of myself as an odd one or different in

any way, not at all, I just had a way, a way that was mine and mine alone. A way that was maybe a bit peculiar but I liked that. I liked the fact that other people weren't odd in the same way, but I felt that being odd suited me better than being popular. My oddness had a certain something, I thought. A style. A style that belonged to me. Then it became a habit and I no longer thought about my odd style, that was how I was and that was that. Different.

Well, maybe.

And there were other girls who were odd ones too and that was how it was. And we loved each other and that was that. I was 18 in May 1968 and it seemed as though my style was becoming popular and that everything was going back to normal, if I dare use that word because I really don't like the word normal. I prefer the word abnormal but only just because in the word abnormal you can still hear the word normal and that's a word I really don't want to hear.

Some words are like that and there's nothing you can do

about it. They stick in the throat. I know the sensation and frankly it's not nice, far from it. Afterwards you have to breathe these long, slow breaths for at least twenty minutes. After twenty minutes if you're really concentrating on your breathing it might pass, but I have trouble breathing like that for so long.

Anyway once my style had become almost fashionable no one could be bothered to comment on it anymore. There's no point in commenting on something that's at the height of fashion. And they stopped bothering to tell me that I should wear the dresses that had never suited me because dresses don't suit my shape. I was always too short for dresses so the waist of the dress would cling to my thighs and it was horrifying, literally horrifying, and I would say OK now you can see that dresses really don't work on me, I should just stick to my own odd style. But it suits you, it really does, if you just get it altered it'll look great. But alterations always end badly and I would be trailing around with something altered and you can always tell when things have been altered and that's worse than anything else.

Sometimes I felt as though it was me that people wanted to alter, just a couple of small changes and everything would be all right, and sometimes I felt the same, that I should make some changes to myself, but there was no point.

She always repeats the same thing and when I tell her, you already told me that, she gets angry.

I'm not even allowed to speak in my own home, you stop me from speaking as soon as I open my mouth.

The next time she repeats herself I don't say anything, I just sigh.

I'm not sure whether she notices or not, I don't know.

She doesn't say anything and continues her story about the taxi and the airport, about a woman who is well off and is in hospital with cancer and about a man who's in hospital because he fell over in his apartment at the age of eighty-six when he'd been managing so well. Now he'll never be the same again. He was still walking without any help, and eating plenty too.

It rains and it rains. Even though it's summer.

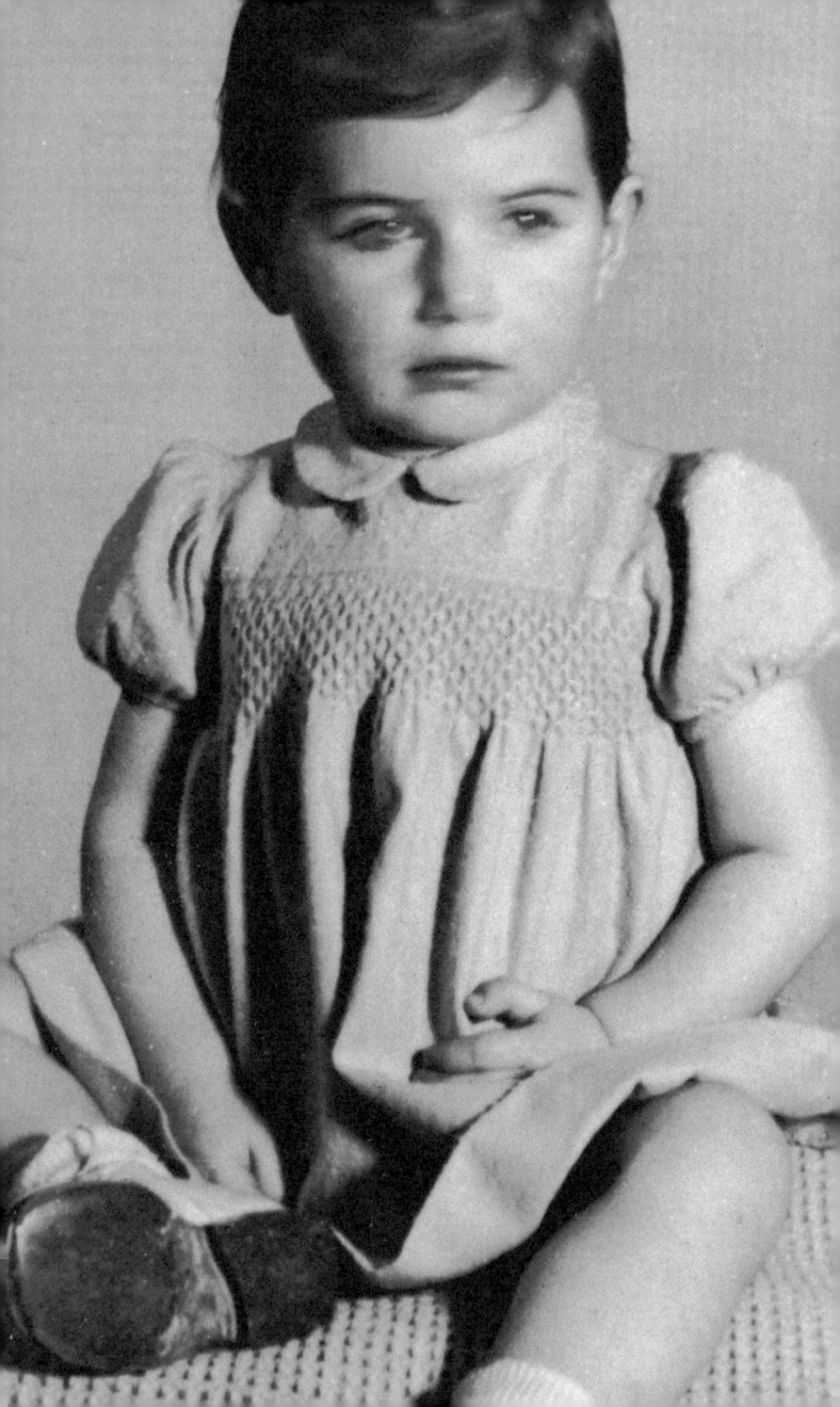

I begin to prepare myself for her death. A friend asks, how are you doing that. I try to imagine myself without her. And I think that it'll be OK.

Not for her. For me. Or the other way round.

But it's meant to be impossible to really prepare yourself so I'm wasting my time.

Anyway, she has this terrifying desire to live.

And what about you? I'm not sure.

She says, they've really conned me this time at the hospital. They told me it'd just be a small operation, nothing serious, but now I realise it's the opposite, that they'll be messing with my heart.

Stop worrying about it.

She sighs and says no.

Then she groans without realising it.

I leave the room.

I come back in and ask her why she's groaning.

Am I groaning. I'm not groaning.

She can't hear her groans.

She waits for the carer to arrive. She always starts waiting early. Hours early, even. And no matter where she's going she always leaves early, even when she's going nowhere, even now she has nowhere to go. Or not often. Anyway, most of the time she stays at home. But even there she starts waiting early. Even when there's nothing to wait for.

She tells me, come, let's talk a little, you never talk to me anymore.

All right, let's talk a little. What about? About anything.
Let's make the shopping list.

I sigh but go and sit opposite her at the kitchen table. It's always in the kitchen that these things happen.

A bag of floury potatoes, fromage blanc, butter. And then she's out of ideas. Fruit, but fruit no longer has any taste. And fromage blanc. You already said that. Yes, but I need fromage blanc and sliced brown bread. I put fromage blanc on my toast with a bit of salt and some pepper and that lasts me all evening.

In the morning too, but then I add a bit of jam. Yes, I knew that already.

I feel the noose start to tighten.

We prepare the list together and she seems happier.

I return to the bedroom where I write.

She enters. Shouts my name. Yes.

We left something off the list, can you add it. I don't remember what it is. I've already forgotten.

And I say automatically, pre-cut vegetables for the soup.
Yes, that's it. I need my soup at lunchtime. Yes.
Now I've lost my thread.
And I need to write.
When I write her groans grow quieter.

Every day a new carer arrives.
Each has their speciality. Each prepares her something to

eat from their home country and my mother is delighted. She's delighted on couscous day. She's delighted on Bolivian speciality day. She's delighted. And each time she says, they do eat well where you come from. I won't ever get to go there, it's a real shame. I used to go to all sorts of countries but mostly just to see family. I wasn't really there to see the place. My daughter on the other hand, she goes all over the place to show her films. She's even been to Japan. She never told me about it. She just said it's far away. As for Cambodia, she just said it's beautiful. I'm sure there's a lot to say about Cambodia and Japan for that matter, but she hardly told me a thing. Except that in Cambodia she caught a virus which she still hasn't shaken off. And as for China, because she's also been to China, her excuse is that she was only there for eight days. It's modern now and there are these big images everywhere. They even project them onto boats, she showed me a video of it. It was taken at night and all you could make out were these images moving across floating boats and then there was a lot of music. I told her that it seemed gay. She said I wouldn't necessarily use that word. Music is gay, it gives things an atmosphere. Yes, well then, I suppose you're right. Anyway, in China she got a tapeworm. I wonder what she could have eaten to have got a tapeworm. She never pays attention so things happen to her all the time, like tapeworms and dirty Cambodian viruses. They told her not to go swimming in the river but she did it anyway.

And then she bumped her head and twisted her ankle. They told her to wear sturdy shoes but she probably forgot.

She's always been this way.

As soon as the carers arrive my mother stops her groaning.

She saves it for me or for herself when she's alone and no longer aware of her surroundings.

When there are people around the groaning stops.

And I start to live again.

Every morning after I wake up I go and stand at her bedroom door to see if she's still breathing.

She's breathing loudly and with difficulty but she's breathing.

Her body looks so small and scrawny over there, wrapped up in a duvet. I feel sick. It wasn't like that before but that's how it is now and I think to myself that one day it'll probably be like that for me too.

She's started to talk in her sleep again. She says, oh no, oh no. Over and over. Then lets out a sort of cry. Then quiet.

I distance myself from her. I go and shut myself in another room, one that's far away. But I can still hear her.

She always leaves the door to her room open.

I'll go and close it.

That's better.

Her sleeping noises are quieter now.

And once again I remind myself that I should prepare for her death. I don't think that she'll die but I should prepare myself just in case.

I try to feel what I would feel if it happened.

I don't feel a thing.

Maybe I'm ready.

Maybe it's because I don't believe it'll happen that I don't feel a thing.

Sometimes she comes into the small room I use to write, the one where I hide to avoid her, she enters it without warning and shouts something. I say to myself, I'm going to kill her.

It would be easy and what is there to prevent me from doing it.

I'm the one preventing myself from doing it.

Then I tell myself that she's entered the room because she wants some human contact and I can understand that perfectly. I've always understood that sort of thing. She's always needed human contact. That's just how she is and it's a good thing.

I tell myself that it's a good thing, a very good thing.

She likes to say how are you and she likes to say I am well. Sometimes I can tell from her voice on the other end of the phone that she's not well but first of all she says, I am well. When I tell her that she doesn't sound like herself she says, I'm just tired. I tell her, you always get tired when the season changes. So we talk about seasons. I think she shouldn't stay in Belgium over the winter because it's a terrible time to be there, but now she doesn't feel she has the strength to travel and I understand that.

I go out with a friend for an hour.

When I come back she says, L. phoned when you were out.

OK, I'll call her back.

L. tells me, your mother thinks you're avoiding her, that you behave like you're in prison.

My mother is right. She's understood. She understands everything.

Did she really use the word prison?

No, she said something else, I can't remember what, but it meant prison. At least that's what I took it to mean.

I found a detective story to take my mind off things. But the story wasn't gripping. It was set in a French village. The streets were damp. I prefer these books to be set in Los Angeles. Los Angeles is bigger, but it's not just that. There are murders, coyotes, highways. Heat.

The landscape is bigger. Less sweaty.

I manage to distance myself. I manage to block out the sound of her moans.

A cousin calls from Canada to say she understands how hard it is, caring for ageing parents. I get a lump in my throat. I barely manage a yes. Then, inaudibly, now's not a good time. Let's speak another time.

But she hasn't heard me. I say it again, barely any louder, let's speak another time.

Suddenly everyone in the family has heard the news.

And everyone says, you should put her in an old people's home.

They're much better these days, you know, in fact they call them retirement homes now and you even get former secretaries of state going to live there.

I say, we'll think about it.

But it's already been thought about, she won't go.

I look at her and know there's no question about it.

She'll never change her mind and so she won't go. No, there's no question about it. My mother, this sack of bones, still feels like a person and she says that old people's homes are a way of getting rid of people, that they're for people waiting for death.

She's not waiting for death. She doesn't want death to arrive. No, there's no question about it.

Anyway, she wouldn't want to leave her apartment.

She likes her apartment. She liked this apartment as soon

as she saw it.

And she still likes it, maybe even more than before. It's the nicest apartment she's ever had and she made sure to buy one with plenty of bedrooms so that she could sometimes have the children to stay. She likes everything about this apartment.

As long as the kitchen is spotless.

But what more do you want from this poor kitchen? It's clean.

Yes, but it has to be spotless.

So I find a cigarette and go and smoke on the balcony.

The ashes drop into the neighbour's garden, the neighbour who lives on the ground floor.

After a sentence that ends in the word spotless, a cigarette on the balcony is the only thing that can save me.

Even then I can still hear her say, spotless, sparkling clean, immaculate.

And I know that she's on about the kitchen again. I can no longer hear the children playing in the garden, I feel as deaf as she is when she says spotless.

She almost managed to stand up almost straight in order to look at the kitchen. Since her return from the hospital, she's had the posture of a puppet.

Sometimes friends arrive. They make conversation. You'll soon be back on your feet. You'll see.

You're already looking better than you did last week.

That's thanks to the hairdresser. It helps. Her three bits of hair have been gathered into a fringe. It makes her look young. It makes her look worse.

Her first outing had been to the hairdresser, which is less than five minutes from her apartment, but because she was having such difficulty walking my sister drove her there and back. They don't have 'hairdressers' there, but 'stylists'. Now she has a stylist who's advised her to grow her hair out and when she returns home from the new stylist she feels great.

Yes, she came home with her hair done. The hairdresser had managed to hide the fact that she only has a few hairs left on her head. I don't know how but the proof is there.

So now she sometimes allows someone or other to visit her in the afternoon for a coffee without feeling embarrassed or ashamed. She's had her hair done.

My sister serves the coffee and cake. She lays the table because my mother is still too weak to do it.

And it's been made clear that it's better for me to do nothing or else it might end in disaster. A real disaster. Like breaking a cup, knocking something over, staining the tablecloth, dropping the tray, or worse.

And the conversation starts up again, but really, you'll feel much better soon. You just need some rest, that's all.

And someone or other always asks, do you have a date for the operation yet?

In a month's time.

A month, someone or other exclaims. These women all know what you don't know. She might not hold out for a month.

And everyone sighs. Everyone knows that anything can happen in a month, including a last breath.

Yesterday on the phone she said, it's a drag, all this waiting.
It really is a drag. I wish it were tomorrow.
I didn't say that after the operation, if she were still alive,

it would be a drag too. That ten days in hospital would be a drag. And that weeks of recovery, what they call rehabilitation, would also be a drag.

I told myself, I won't be there for that.
 I don't want to be there to help with her recovery.
 I'm no help anyway. You do me more harm than good, that's what she said. Go home. That's not exactly how she'd said it but that's what she'd meant, or at least that's what I'd taken her to mean.
 Sometimes I get things the wrong way round but not always. She'd also said something I'm sure of, when you're here I can feel you running away from me, that I annoy you. Just tell me if I annoy you. But I'd said no, it's not that. She'd sounded like she really wanted to know. That tone of voice was one I'd never heard before.
 My mother is changing. I'm not. I won't tell her that she's annoying me, that's not how I speak to my mother. I don't think I ever cried or shouted when I was little, or even when I wasn't. Either I didn't want to or I wasn't able to and I think that's because of what happened to my mother before I was born.
 I've just got other things on my mind, I replied, decisions I have to make that I'm worried about.
 Just make them, don't fret about it. No, I reply.
 And I can't even manage to write.
 Well you know I can't help you with that, I'm no writer.

One day, sometime after, when she'd just come home after a few weeks in hospital in Mexico, my sister said to me, she doesn't even take an interest in anything anymore and nothing we do is ever enough.
 No, she's not interested in anything anymore and she hurts all over, that's the only thing she's interested in and I

can understand her. Even though it's not very interesting, it still somehow is. She's crippled with arthritis, her hands hurt, her shoulders too, and her eyes and her stomach. Her stomach is bloated, there's air in it. She has trouble digesting anything. She's weak, she can barely walk. She needs help showering.

She would love to take a bath but she can't, she wouldn't be able to get out afterwards.

Before she had a bath every day and it would relax her, for a little while afterwards she'd feel better.

But now all that is over, truly over. That was before, not so long ago, but before she flew business class to Mexico for her granddaughter's wedding.

It was after the operation and the doctor who told her, now you can travel and walk. Walking is very important. That's what everyone says. But a year after the operation she'd fallen out of bed and could no longer take a bath.

The wedding was the beginning of the end. After the wedding she went into hospital in Mexico for a few weeks.

That should have been the end.

My brother-in-law said, your mother is strong, very strong.

He was the one who called me in New York to tell me I should come and say goodbye to my mother. He called me in New York because that was where I was living at the time with C.

Once again I had moved cities to have a new life. I'm on my way, I said. C. asked me if I'd like her to come with me. I said no, now's not the right time. Another time. But it was never the right time and C. never came with me to stay in my sister's house in Mexico.

I went to the bank to change some money and by the time I got to the front of the queue I had tears in my eyes. The cashier, who was from somewhere in South America, looked at me with such kindness that I told her all about my mother. She comforted me and I felt better. I slept the whole flight.

Though I did have to wonder how the kindness of a stranger could have such an effect.

My brother-in-law came to get me from the airport. I spotted him at arrivals straight away. But I couldn't tell from his expression whether she was still alive. We hugged each other and he said, let's go.

We drove in silence. I was cold. There was no traffic. It was night time. It was very dark. Do you want me to turn the heat on? If you want. No, actually, I'm fine.

When we arrived at the hospital we took the lift up to her room. Or maybe we didn't. I can't remember. Maybe her room was on the ground floor, I can no longer remember.

We found a woman who told us, you can't go in yet. It's not allowed. The woman had to make a call to get permission.

She didn't manage to get hold of anyone and asked us to wait. But we couldn't take it. We paced up and down in front of her and my brother-in-law kept asking her to call again. She kept saying, I'll try in five minutes.

Finally, the double doors opened automatically to let someone out of A&E. We took this as our cue to sneak in. The woman shouted at us. We didn't pay any attention. We turned left onto another corridor. We were lost. No one was around. We didn't know what to do. Suddenly my brother-in-law spotted the room in the dark. He has a brilliant sense of direction, even when there's no light. We had to put on a mask straight away, or maybe after, I don't know. I can't remember. There were tubes everywhere. And wires. Machines that bleeped. An oxygen mask.

When I approached the bed she opened one eye. She was alive.

She was still alive. And that's when she said you were aggressive with me. My brother-in-law looked at me and said, she's not herself. But I knew it wasn't that.

It was the opposite, she was telling her truth. Without saying I love you. The moment had arrived. I'd forgotten all the other times in Brussels. The smack, the you keep running away from me, the you do me more harm than good. I'd forgotten all those times. The ones that had suddenly allowed me to breathe.

I had forgotten them but afterwards I remembered and I was happy.

My mother was saying what she really meant. I was terribly happy. I said to myself, she's changing and if she does pull through she won't be the same person and nor will I. Well, maybe.

I don't remember what I said to her.

Probably just see you tomorrow because I was staying

in Mexico for a few days and I would be coming back the next day.

But really, I didn't want to engage with what she had said to me. I should have said, you're right, I was aggressive, but it wasn't the right time. I probably should have said it anyway.

I think I may have even lowered my head.

We sat in silence for a moment.

Then my brother-in-law said, come on, let's go.

Her eyes had shut again as soon as she'd spoken to me. But you could see her breathe through the oxygen mask. She was breathing easily.

It must have done her good to tell me, you were aggressive with me. She seemed to be in peace.

She was living. For how much longer we didn't know.

The next day they put her in a new room. She was no longer in A&E but intensive care.

My sister spoke to the doctors in Spanish. They couldn't give her any news. They were doing all they could. They just said, she's weak. Probably so we wouldn't raise our hopes, not yet, it was too soon. We looked them straight in the eye to see if they were trying to hide something from us.

But they were used to this sort of thing and their eyes gave nothing away.

In my sister's house life went on. That's how it is, life goes on. My sister said, she'll pull through. Yes, probably. She's strong, she's very strong, she doesn't want to die. No. And the next day she was still there, alive.

One day she said, I want to go to Italy. I'd like to buy some new tablecloths. We're running out of tablecloths. They sell them on the beach in Italy.

Afterwards she asked why the doctors didn't speak French. That's how it is here, maman, we're in Mexico. Here you say graçias.

She repeated graçias several times before falling back to sleep but she didn't look like she knew what she was saying.

So my sister said, why don't we go get a coffee. There's no point waiting here.

In the hospital café, a brightly-lit café, I ordered an omelette, juice and cake, I was so desperate to eat. But when the omelette arrived I started to retch. My mother used to say, your eyes are bigger than your belly. But this time it was my sister who said it before adding, just drink some water and then let's go. Where, I asked. Back home. We can come back later, my sister said. Yes, later, I said. She's going to pull through, you'll see, my sister said. I replied with a faint yes. I'm sure of it, my sister said. Why not, I thought, especially if she's already thinking about Italian tablecloths. Why is that anyway? It's the morphine, my sister replied. You think about things like that when you're on morphine. I didn't know that. You think about lots of things when you're on morphine, my sister said. I know that because of my teeth. OK, I said, but I still didn't see what the Italian tablecloths had to do with all of this.

Nor what was she saying graçias for. She kept saying it.

My sister said to me, she was happy in Italy so she remembers it. Everyone, all her friends, were still alive and we all went there together even though dad didn't have much money at the time and it was our first holiday outside Belgium.

I remember that holiday in Italy too, I kept looking out of the window expecting to see P. P. was my best friend at school. I don't know why I did that because I knew that P. wasn't going to be in Italy.

She's going to pull through, my sister kept saying, and I said, yes, I believe you and anyway I'm ready. But what will we do if the worst happens?

We'd have to send the casket back to Brussels. We both sigh. Come on, let's go.

When we arrived home the dog came to greet us in a frenzy, running around in every direction like a spinning top.

I picked him up and laughed. He's the kind of dog that makes you laugh.

Such a little dog, a Pomeranian spitz, could make anyone laugh.

So my sister begins to laugh too. And even the maids start to laugh.

Everyone laughs. Nobody remembers why.

We all have tears in our eyes.

The table is set.

My sister can't take it anymore.

No one can take it anymore. Silence has set in.

But my sister wants to have fun, to invite people over. My sister wants noise.

My nephew wants to go out. He wants to dance all night and drink and maybe even meet a girl and kiss her all night long.

I'd like to be like him or my sister but I can't manage it so I decide to take a sleeping pill.

Already, my sister says. Don't take one today. Stay with us. Don't take one. So I don't and instead I take my sister in my arms.

My nephew asks how his grandmother is doing. My sister says, she's still with us, she's talking about Italian tablecloths and keeps saying graçias.

She probably thinks she's in Italy, my nephew says. She likes Italy, she told me so.

She told me that she prefers Italy to Mexico and that if we'd settled in Italy she would have come to visit us more often and would have felt that she was less far away. She feels far away from everyone she loves and she would have much preferred that no one had gone to live so far away. Everyone is far away now. The family is dotted all round the world, there's hardly anyone left in Belgium. There are cousins living in Miami Beach among palm trees, others in Los Angeles, next to the sea, others in the suburbs of Toronto, others in South Africa and elsewhere. Others in Israel. We've lost track of some of them.

Don't you ever wonder where they are and if they're still alive? Of course they are, why wouldn't they be? We've just lost track of them.

My nephew asks why we haven't bothered to look for them.

My sister replies that we wouldn't know how to go about it.

Well you could hire a private detective. Yes, we could.

We don't because we know that there's no point, though we'd never say that.

One day my mother told me about her cousin and her mother, that her mother was very modern and that an older male cousin had come to live with them. They went to the Gymnasium together. One day my grandmother came home to find her daughter, my mother, crying in the kitchen. Her mother asked my mother, who must have been about ten, why she was crying like that, and she said, because I love my cousin. I'm so in love with my cousin it hurts. My grandmother said, well everybody loves your cousin, he's wonderful, but he's your cousin. See how modern she was? I didn't really understand the story but I said yes, I can see that. And then I asked, and what happened to this cousin? Did he disappear along with all the others that stayed over there? She let out a sigh.

Do you still think about him sometimes, your cousin? Yes, but as little as possible. Otherwise I start to think about all the others. You know, we had a big family, over there in Poland, a very big family. That's how it was then. We were all very big families. That's probably why your father wanted a third child. But I refused. I had two girls and that was enough for me, especially with you giving me so many worries. Of course you were a lovely girl and beautiful too with your blue eyes. People would come up to the pram just to look at your eyes. And they would compliment me. But a third child, no. Giving birth was terrible and even afterwards it was difficult, especially when you refused to eat and cried all night with your nightmares.

You'd never want to tell me your dreams in the morning but I've always loved telling people my dreams. My dreams make me think I'm living a double life. But when I asked you to tell me what happened in your dreams or your nightmares you'd say, I can't remember them, but I could see from the fear on your face that you could remember them perfectly well, but still you'd say, I don't have dreams, I never have.

Of course in the daytime you didn't have nightmares and so you'd run around in every direction, especially when it was time to eat.

You used to say that you didn't want to eat because the food got stuck in your throat.

The only thing you would eat, and even then we could never be sure, were meatballs in tomato sauce with pasta.

And you'd get it everywhere so we'd have to change your clothes.

Your sister had no problem eating, though she would eat very slowly. It'd take her hours just to finish her bottle. But she always did. And she was a good sleeper too, so I was less worried about her.

I'm going to go and see her, my nephew announced. Don't wear her out, she's struggling. She needs all her energy. Does anyone want to come with me?

We're going later.

Later when we got there she was tossing and turning in her sleep. She was saying something but we couldn't understand what. Unintelligible words and sentences. My sister said again, it's the morphine.

Why does she need so much morphine? Where does she hurt? I don't know, everywhere.

My sister wanted to check her out of the hospital, she thinks that it's not doing her any good and that she would feel better at home. My sister asked the doctor who dropped by for a few seconds a day.

The doctor said that being there is doing her good and that if we took her home she'd die.

And if she stays here? Here she might not, the doctor said in Spanish. She's responding well to the antibiotics. So why is she delirious? Well because that's how it is. Will she always be like that from now on? No, just for the moment, the doctor said.

She's dreaming, that's all.

The doctor wanted to get on because a woman who'd been attacked had just been brought in.

My sister asked, is it serious. The doctor said, I don't think we'll be able to save her but you never know. We see it all the time. That's just how it is. There's not much we can do about it.

My sister said, murderers never get arrested here. They're stronger than the police.

The doctor said, probably.

Then he left.

My sister said, let's go and get some sleep. Yes. Let's go.

It's the morning and I hear my nephew come in from the nightclub.

I'd like to be like him, I'd like to go dancing with him.

I go and tell my sister this, she shrugs. I don't think he'd like that. He goes dancing with people his own age. Yes, of course, I say. He must see me as an old woman, sometimes instead of calling me by my first name he even calls me aunty and because I grew up with my mother's aunts and used to call them the three aunts, I've always thought of aunts as old. Anyway the three aunts aren't around anymore and my mother has no more aunts.

But we still talk about those aunts, we think about them sometimes, often even. At least, my mother and I talk about them and we laugh. And about my father too but we laugh less. I don't know why.

My mother thinks that he's still looking out for her, even though he's dead. I always say yes. Yes, he probably is.

I told my sister what my mother had said to me the night I arrived because I couldn't stop thinking about it, I had to tell her that she had only opened her eyes to tell me that I'd been aggressive with her, and that was all she'd said to me. My sister said again, she's not herself, don't think about it. OK, I said.

At the wedding, or rather after the wedding when we were eating and drinking, and my mother was refusing to dance, even though she'd always enjoyed dancing at weddings and other places too, I lit a cigarette and my mother snapped, don't smoke, and I snapped back, don't tell me what to do, and I went and smoked. That's what my mother was remembering. That's why she'd said, you were aggressive with me, that's what she'd said as soon as she'd recognised me in the semi-darkness of the hospital room.

Later, after she was released from hospital she told me she couldn't remember anything, but still took me through the details of what had happened and how Clara and I had carried her upstairs to her bedroom because she could no longer walk, then how she'd gone to hospital and there they spotted her pulmonary embolism, and that the doctors weren't sure whether she would survive. I said you've had a lucky escape and you're going to start feeling better, bit by bit.

She didn't feel she was getting any better.

Yes, I promise you're getting better, I know because I haven't seen you for a few weeks and I can tell you you're unrecognisable. You don't even need oxygen anymore.

Before you needed oxygen all the time and now not at all, and that's a change, a change for the better, and your cheeks have got their colour back. Do you really think so, she said. Yes. And it was true.

Before I left, C. had said to me, you know that your mother might die. Yes. She might.

C. always spoke truthfully and what she said was true. My mother might well have died and even though I had said I was ready I don't really think I was.

C. knew about the death of a mother. But whenever someone asked her about it she would say no comment. Always no comment except once.

When I arrived in Mexico for the wedding I got a shock seeing my mother. I said to my sister, she looks like she's aged about twenty years in a few weeks, how is that possible.

She looked green and thin and she seemed to be aware of it but in spite of everything she'd tried to put on a good face for the wedding. You can't age twenty years when your granddaughter is about to get married and you certainly can't be green. You have to be overjoyed. One day her granddaughter will have a child and she'll have to be overjoyed. Get dressed, put on some make-up.

Be overjoyed.

Someone has to help her get dressed because with her broken shoulder she can't do it by herself.

Luckily it's her left shoulder. And there was nothing that could be done for this shoulder. Her bones were like sand and they wouldn't have been able to hold a screw even if they'd put one in. That's what the doctor told me.

I didn't know what to say, so I said, but she will still be able to use her left arm, won't she. Yes, but not like before.

He looked at me but didn't respond, he just repeated not like before, I said OK, well don't operate then.

I was wrong and now there's nothing that can be done and she can't use her left arm at all and anyway they should have suggested prosthetics, not screws, but I didn't learn that until much later.

Anyway, this doctor turned out to be an idiot but I remember reading somewhere that idiots are victims too.

When she woke up, I said, you're not 18 anymore. When you wake up in the middle of the night to go to the toilet put on the light and get out of bed carefully.

I can see, I don't need the light on. I can see because the headlamps from the cars on the street come into the dining room. No, you still have to put the light on.

When I said you're not 18 anymore I could see her world fall apart. She refused to eat or drink, and in the evening and the morning when I went to see her because I was working during the day and work is important to me, I could see that she was letting herself go, that she'd decided not to resist any longer. What's the point when you're not 18 anymore. Quite simply, she was letting herself die.

I thought, maybe she knows what she's doing.

And it carried on like that for the rest of the week.

My sister was arriving on Friday so on Thursday she started to eat again. She was scared of my sister. She knew that my sister wouldn't let her carry on like that, that my sister wouldn't let her die. So she started eating again. She hated the hospital food so me and my cousin bought her liquid food replacement from the pharmacy and she drank it. She drank it slowly but she drank it.

I thought to myself, it's only when I'm around that she wants to die.

I thought to myself, maybe now she's accepted the fact that she's not 18 anymore and it had to happen in the end and it wasn't so bad, not really. My mother is someone who likes to please. And that has something to do with when she was 18. But you can please at any age. Or nearly. With her bandaged fist, her broken shoulder and everything that hurt it would be more difficult but it could still happen. Especially when it came to the paramedics who were strong and handsome.

She had probably already started to think about how she could still please beautiful young people. And she was probably also scared of my sister who was about to arrive so she started to eat again.

I told her that it was great she was eating. She barely responded.

She had to put on make-up for the wedding. She made

herself up but she looked worse. The blusher on her cheeks made her look even older. It made things worse but I didn't say anything.

My mother said to me, you could do with some make-up too. Yes.

She'll never let go. Until the day she dies this is the sort of thing she'll say.

I said to myself that it was probably a good sign, that it was probably the reason she was still alive. Maybe that's why my brother-in-law had said your mother is strong, very strong.

I wondered whether it was a good thing, to be so strong.

Everyone, or at least my brother-in-law and possibly my sister too, told me it's because she's a survivor, she learned how to survive and she must have been strong to have done so.

I'd had enough of all these stories about survivors. For years that was all I could think about. Now I'd had enough. Really enough. I said to myself that maybe my having enough was the start of my healing process because I was ill too. And I still am. It's a recurrent, chronic illness. I take medicine for my mood every day. It's my mood that's ill. When I'm in too good a mood I have to be careful. I have to get rid of my too good mood quickly or else I'll end up in hospital like her, or they'll lock me up. If I have no mood at all, no desire for anything which means I don't see anyone and no one sees me, I know I won't be locked up. I'd been naive in thinking that by being fed up with thinking about survivors and non-survivors I could manage my moods and my illness. But then I read that that wasn't possible, that my illness had developed from early infancy when I didn't realise I had a father, or maybe my mother hadn't let me realise I had one, because maybe my

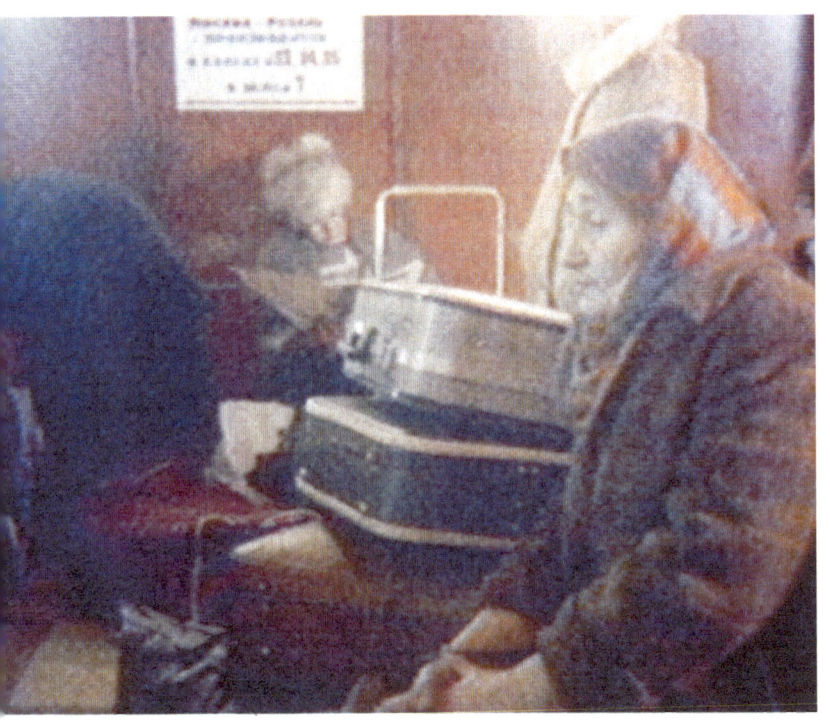

mother and I were too bonded, a bond that was fatal for me. That isn't strictly true because when I was little I always said that I would like to marry a man like my father. No, it wasn't strictly true but that didn't change anything.

And it wasn't a hole in my body that could eventually be stitched up, it was the tissue itself that was irreparable and there was nothing I could do about it. So I could continue to think about survivors and those who died but I don't anymore, except when my brother-in-law makes me. Or when someone else does. Or when something else does.

The conditions are always right for thinking about it again, even words or things that could just as easily make you think of something else. There are many examples of these words, for example when someone says to me that the air is pure or when someone says that something is crawling with lice, or even when someone mentions a crisis point, before adding, like in 1933. Or even more benign things that I can't remember right now. The word remember too, and the word memory. We have so many duties now. We have a duty to ourselves not to smoke, and the word smoke also makes me shudder. As well as the word field and the word earth.

Well there's a whole series of words like that, like Christmas and New Year, but that's a different kind of shudder.

And also Santa, high in the sky, come down the chimney, don't be shy, sometimes even the word sky sends a shiver down my spine, even though I like the sky, I like every kind of sky, especially when you can see a lot of it. I like the sky so much that I can stay in bed for hours in my Paris apartment just looking at it.

Everyone says, you're very lucky to be able to see the sky from your bed, and I agree with them.

In New York I have to crick my neck to see just a bit of sky even though I live in Harlem. As soon as I get to Harlem I want to go back to Paris and after a few days in Paris I want to be somewhere else, even Harlem would do but also elsewhere, though I can never tell where. But I'll go back to New York anyway. Yes, I'll go because it was me who brought C. there and it had become unbearable.

I had insomnia and I was crying all the time. It was unbearable.

Even so, C. encouraged me to say what I really felt and so I said yes, this is what I want. It will be good and it's really what I want. She wants the best for me and that's what she gives me. She would say to me, stop being a child, that's enough now.

Yes, I knew it was enough but I couldn't shake it off.
Not fully in any case.
And most of the time I didn't speak at all. I refused,

sometimes I would try but I would rarely succeed.

If there hadn't been this emphasis on saying what I really felt my relationship with C. probably wouldn't have lasted as long as it did, but I had the feeling that all her questioning forced me out of myself and that it was a good thing.

But instead of saying what I really felt, I just said things badly. I said horrible things to her and to those closest to me, things that I didn't really feel. Destruction for destruction's sake. I was proud of it, and then I regretted it.

Deep down I knew that isn't how you say what you really feel and that you can criticise others without being horrible, by being measured and kind. But in the period when I said what I really felt badly, I said such horrible things that afterwards I got ill.

So each time I'd fall back into the habit of keeping things bottled up and my anger went back to being the kind that killed me slowly.

But then someone said to me, it's clear from your films that you put your whole self into them. I hadn't realised that because I didn't think I knew even a part of myself, let alone my whole self. And whenever I finished a film I felt that I'd only left a small trace. I needed to leave a trace, really I did. But my body's tissue was still rotten.

I liked making films but whenever I heard people talking about me using my full name I knew that they were talking about someone who hadn't just left some kind of trace but someone who had made something more like a body of work. And I didn't want to contradict them. No, certainly not. I didn't want to tell them that they were just traces so I told them nothing at all.

My mother creates a feeling of unbearable anxiety for everyone around her and we run away from her so that we don't catch it but somehow we still do and my mother can sense that we're running away from her, that we're treating her like a piece of furniture, well not like a piece of furniture exactly, or not like a piece of furniture at all, but sometimes she picks up on what we feel so her anxiety mounts and we end up running even further away.

My sister says, just ignore it. You have to ignore it, I ignore it. I come and go as I please, I don't tell her where I'm going or give her my mobile number.

My mother would like nothing more than to call my sister. Why do you want to call her, she's at work. Leave her be. Yes, but I'd like to know when she's coming home.

She'll be back for lunch. OK, but I'd still like to speak to her.

OK, let me call her. It's engaged. My mother wrings her hands.

But what about D.? D. is my nephew, her grandson. What about D., when will he be home? He comes and goes as he pleases, he never says where he's going. He treats this place like a hotel.

But maman, he's not a child anymore.

Well, I'm not coming back here again. A phrase that falls like a guillotine's blade. It's true, she won't come to Mexico again.

She'll go home to Brussels, at least at sea level she can breathe more easily than in Mexico which is high up and in Brussels maybe she will feel better. In any case that's what we make her believe and we try to believe it and she tries too. And she walks with the nurse who holds onto her arm, until she reaches the garden where she'll sit in the sun.

Here in Mexico she's only left the house three times. She says it resentfully.

But maman, you can't even stand up straight.

That's not what she means. I know what she means but I don't let on. Here she's no longer in control of her own life. People come and go around her. But she stays with the nurse.

The nurse doesn't let her out of her sight and she can't even have a bath anymore. The nurse washes and showers her. She used to love having a bath in the morning, it was one of her greatest pleasures. Now she doesn't even have that.

Today she doesn't want to shower, it tires her out.

I say, have one tomorrow, you're not dirty anyway.

But my sister wants her to have one. She doesn't want her to mope around in her dressing gown all day. It'd be better for her.

My sister can't bear my mother moping around in her dressing gown. And the dressing gown is lopsided because of her broken shoulder.

I don't know why but her broken shoulder is more obvious when she's in her dressing gown. And when I ask my sister, what are we going to do about this broken shoulder, she says, there's nothing more we can do. Let's not talk about it, she's not thinking about it anymore anyway. We just have to help her get dressed and that's it, it's not really that bad. Not really that bad, but what is that bad? You can still live with a broken shoulder. You can eat, you can sleep.

Even with a broken heart, with deformed hands, you can live with these.

My mother says, your sister orders me around you know. I'm not allowed to do what I want around here because she gets angry.

I'm eating, you know, I'm eating often. Yes, I tell her, you're doing much better, better than a month ago, even.

It'll take some time. You were very ill but you'll recover. Look, you're already recovering. As usual, I was already desperate to leave and at that time leaving meant returning to Harlem.

But since C. and I have been in Harlem I've been unable to write more than a line. So why leave? I'm not saying that C. prevents me from writing or that I prevent her from writing, after all she's the one who has to write a book, but there's something that prevents both of us when we're together.

Even though both of us would like the other to write and to be happy. But what happens is always the opposite. I can't even make notes anymore. And the only thing I want to write about, but that I never end up writing about, is the fact I find it harder to hear people with high-pitched voices and that sometimes I find it hard to understand anything at all.

I feel like I'm trapped in a fishing net which gets tighter every day and the tighter it gets the harder it is to love.

Is it possible that one day I might ask, where's the net gone, and find that I miss it.

I hope not, but you never know. I've always created these prisons for myself. And the net is just one more, so how could I not end up missing it. But I can feel this one even more than the other ones, the ones I've got used to.

And to think it had all started so well. I even told her one day that I was happy.

Now I try to tell her, loosen the net, let me breathe a bit, you're hurting us both. I want to end it but I don't know how. I come, I go, I hide, I lie. Afterwards I don't even remember what I've said but she knows, she remembers everything I've said and even the things I haven't. Every word, every breath, every silence, every lowered or turned head, every I don't know why I can't sleep, I don't know why I wake up crying. And I tell her again that it's true, I don't know why. And there's a part of me that's telling the truth, a part of me that doesn't know, not fully anyway.

And she tells me with her unfaltering memory, you told me last week (on Tuesday) that you had a feeling you knew why you weren't sleeping. And I say, I don't remember. I don't remember what I said to you.

She doesn't believe me and she tells me so. You do know. I defend myself and dig myself an even bigger hole.

She's so perceptive that every time I try to get out of something with a tender word or a gesture that will make us forget all that, it ends up coming to the surface and it's even worse.

So now I've stopped trying to get out of things and I stay quiet. But that's worse. It's bad and it gets even worse every day.

She was sitting or lying on the horrible black plastic sofa where she's reading or trying to. I don't know.

Now I don't remember the sofa as being so terrible but at the time I hated it.

She was reading or trying to but I had the feeling that she wasn't reading much at all and was watching me instead, I don't know why. Well, I do a bit. She was probably on high alert.

She was probably imagining that I'd leave her there, that I'd abandon her.

So she'd decided to watch me. To scrutinise my every

movement. I willed her to read, to write. Don't spend your time worrying about me.

She said, you come and go because you don't want to spend your time at home with me, and there was a bit of truth in that. It was the truth.

As soon as I woke up I looked for something to do to get myself out of the house so that she couldn't spend the day watching me. I didn't actually want to go out, I had caught a virus, my stomach hurt, I wasn't sleeping at night. I would have preferred to stay at 527 West. I couldn't bring myself to stay at home. No. I didn't feel at home except for very occasionally. Yes, occasionally we'd sleep in each other's arms and this would give us a moment of respite but then it would start again because if I ever managed to sleep I would wake up in tears.

And the questions would start again, why are you crying, I don't know.

You do know. No. Sometimes I cry, that's all.

No.

I tried to wriggle free. Sometimes I stopped trying. I suffocated.

She would look at me with her dark, earnest eyes, she would look at me and I'd think she could see right through me. She'd hold her gaze on me for so long that I would try to breathe through it and forget that it was there.

One day I said to my best friend in New York, we're going to end up killing each other. I was trying to explain what had happened to see if there was a right or wrong in this story.

C. had almost managed to convince me intellectually that when I called someone from before, from before her, I was doing something wrong. That when I closed my laptop when she came into the room, it was to hide what I was writing from her. But it wasn't true. And I wasn't even writing. I explained to her that it was just a reflex but she didn't believe me. So I spent some time thinking about it and trying to work out whether it really was a reflex. And I concluded that yes, it was. Sometimes I tried to prove to her that I often did things without thinking but that was even worse so I shut up. I ended up speaking less and less to try and put an end to the horrible reproaches that I could never really understand.

And so she reproached me for not speaking.

I tried to say something, I searched for the words, I couldn't find them.

So I let silence linger.

And the darker the apartment was the louder the silence.

My mother kept asking me for the details of what had happened to her. She said she needed to put the pieces back together and in the right order. She thought she would feel better if she had the whole story.

You had a close shave, you were hanging on by a thread. Oh really. Tell me what happened. I tell her. She says, really. Asks for more details. Asks again. Then she says, I can't remember the story.

I can't remember it, how quickly one forgets. There are some things I prefer to forget but not this story. This story is missing. As soon as I know it I'll be able to forget it but before that I want to be able to remember it but I can't. It's driving me mad.

So I try and piece the details together and I realise that I've forgotten them too and that I never fully understood how one day she was at home and the next she was in

A&E. But my mother absolutely has to know. So I say you must have picked something up on the plane. People are always picking things up on planes. And you don't have to remember everything. You're here and that's all that matters. And we think, or at least I think, yes but at what price. With dead, joyless eyes. I wonder, should she really have been brought back from the dead. But she was the one who wanted to live. Everyone says it, she's strong. And I'm the one who sits looking at this poor scrawny being, crazy with worry.

We put an armchair out in the sunny part of the garden for her, we put a big straw hat on her head, and from afar it looks like paradise (idyllic, even). She's old, yes, but she takes pleasure in the sun, in her children, in her grandchildren.

But the children and the grandchildren come and go, hello goodbye, are you leaving already, yes I've got to go to work and you're off as well. Yes.

And I ask, wouldn't you like to read a bit, no my eyes are all blurry. And as for listening to music, my hearing aid has damaged my left ear canal, the canal is too narrow. This hearing aid has caused me a lot of damage. Look how red my ear is. It'll heal. My mother says, yes, maybe, but it's been like this for ages. It'll heal by itself like everything else, but healing now takes longer and longer. Nobody wants to hear it so everyone leaves and she stays at home with the nurse who can't speak French. And with me when I'm there for two or three days.

It's my brother-in-law who says it the most, but sometimes it's the driver too and even the others like the nurse, the nurse who doesn't let my mother out of her sight. Everyone says it, she's very strong.

Now my mother has had enough of this nurse, I can see that, and she's also had enough of people telling her she's so strong all the time when she feels so weak. But she doesn't say anything because she isn't at home. And because when she says something we don't always listen. Everyone knows better than she does when it comes to what's best for her. So the nurse even sleeps in the same room. My mother says, it's weird to wake up with a nurse in the next bed, a nurse who doesn't speak French.

The nurse would like to learn it but that doesn't happen overnight. So they've found other ways of understanding each other. But my mother would prefer a nurse who spoke French. At least then she could talk to them.

But that's how it is and in the morning it's not so bad because in the morning she cries out with hunger and in this house everyone sleeps late, even the maids, so the nurse brings her some coffee and cornflakes and that calms her down. Sometimes she even manages to get back to sleep, that way she wakes up again at the same time as everyone else, when there's some noise in the house, and usually my sister comes to see whether she's slept well and says, maman get up now, don't stay in bed all day. Don't worry, I'm getting up.

But you know even the shoulder that isn't broken is starting to hurt me. Yes, it's because the two shoulders are unbalanced, there's one that hangs lower than the other. Are you in pain? Not really, but I feel like I have one dead shoulder. Yes, but when you're back in Brussels you'll see your physiotherapist and he'll help with that. Yes, my mother loves her physiotherapist and it's no wonder.

She'll go home to Brussels. For the moment she can't, she's still too weak, but soon.

She really wants to although she's scared of being alone, but mostly she would love to be at home and do whatever she wants.

But for the moment she can't do anything by herself. Her hands tremble, she can barely control her legs. You have to build up your muscles, maman, you have to walk. I'm already walking a little, I can walk for five minutes. And tomorrow you'll walk for six and the next day seven. She nods, yes. Yes, probably.

When she goes to sit down either she needs help, usually from the nurse, or she lets herself fall down into the chair. What else can you do without muscles. You must eat more protein, maman. We inject her with vitamin B12 and sometimes even give her blood transfusions to help with the anaemia.

One evening my sister comes to see me in the bedroom where I sleep, her daughter's old bedroom, the one who's just got married. As usual, I'm getting ready for bed early to avoid life. My sister wants to speak to me. She can't take it anymore and I can see why.

We both try to remember whether she's always been like this, so self-involved, fundamentally egotistical, that sort of thing. Or something else.

We can't remember. We can't remember the good times anymore. We can't remember how our mother was before.

We can't remember how she looked after us. We can't remember the fact that it was thanks to her that there was joy in our house.

We can't remember that she came to pick us up from school every day, that she protected us, that she fought for us. We can't remember those things.

Nor the fact that one day she had to go to a department store without telling my father, because I'd stolen something. And that this had humiliated her. And not even the fact that she had put aside money each month so she could send me twenty dollars the first time I ran off to New York.

And suddenly I remember, and it's a horrible memory. I remember the time she came with my father to see me in the clinic where I'd been locked up. I could see them

walking side by side in the fog of the big park. They looked so small in the fog.

When I'd seen them like that, from a distance, I thought to myself, I'll put on a brave face.

I knew that they were struggling. That they were struggling with having a daughter who was locked up in a clinic. Yes, I had to put on a brave face. I didn't tell my sister that story.

They talked to the doctor. The doctor's surname was Pastorale and he wore a leather tie.

And I said to him, that's not your real name, you're hiding your real name in the French soil, in the pastoral landscape. And I added, while I played with his tie, but I can tell you're not from the countryside. And then I said as if by accident but not really, did you know that the Germans made lamps with the skin of the Jews they killed?

So they took everything away from me, my scissors and things that were like scissors, anything that was pointy, and they locked me away.

At night I wanted to leave my room to take a walk in the corridor. I'd really had enough of this room. I tried to open the door. No way of opening it. I remember thinking to myself, there must be some sort of knack to it that I'm not getting because I'm not a practical person. But I knew perfectly well that the door had been locked. I was locked up and that was all there was to it. I thought to myself, I shouldn't have said anything to Doctor Pastorale or talked to him about the Jews. I thought to myself, but surely they don't have the right to do this. This is a step too far. I didn't come here to be locked up, I came here to feel better and because feeling trapped is part of my problem I'm going to feel worse.

As soon as the sun rose I called my doctor at home. Luckily the phone was still working. He got me out of that room. They gave me a room overlooking the park with a door that opened out onto it and they say air is good for you, fresh country air, for example, but often I'm disappointed by the countryside. I can't remember whether they gave me back my scissors. Either way I soon returned to Brussels via the big foggy park and that's where I stayed for a long time, with my father. That's how I got to know him and learned to love him. And it's no wonder.

MY MOTHER LAUGHS

CHANTAL AKERMAN

One day my mother said to me, as I was leaving that place I realised that my heart had died. Maybe it was already slightly dead when I was growing up, or maybe it had always been that way, but I don't think so. Anyway, I'll never know. And what use is there in knowing. It's probably useful when you're trying to work out if your lover means what they say, yes, sometimes it's useful, maybe often, even. But sometimes it's not.

Apart from that she didn't say anything about that place even when I asked her, except for things like, a friend saved my life when she went and stole some potatoes. She only told me the best bits. Apart from the best bits she couldn't say anything.
My mother knows that my sister is protecting herself and that I have difficulty with that.

She knows that my sister is doing everything she can to keep her alive, with no expense spared. Everything except listening to her, everything except taking her in her arms, and that's what my mother wants and needs most, for someone to hold her against their body so that she can forget herself, or the opposite, so that she can feel alive.

Is that what I'm like too, I don't think so. Then why did I decide to go and see C. one day in London. Yes, why if not to be in someone else's arms and arms that I didn't even know, except by emails and texts and messages on Facebook. Yes, I could imagine them and it was overwhelming. These arms should have stayed in my imagination, deep down that's better for me especially when things start the way they did. But it was the first time. I'd never experienced something like this before so I let my guard down and I trusted her.

I said to my sister, you should never have put me on Facebook.

My sister said, I didn't put you on Facebook for that to happen.

I know, but that's what's happened and it's hard to undo.

For you, maybe, replied my sister who has been married for more than thirty years.

She said it to me very kindly. This kindness was moving and I wanted to cry. I said to her, you look very pretty today. Your dress is very beautiful. You think so? I said yes and then, you know I still have some good days.

Luckily. And don't you think maman is doing better, she's not had a good day yet, I mean not a truly good day, but she's doing better. Yes, that's true. But she's speaking less than before, speaking tires her out. Sometimes she talks and for now that makes it a good day.

One morning she talked to me for a long time. And I replied, though I don't remember what. Sometimes the words she says don't matter. The only thing that matters is the response to the thing that isn't expressed. So I tell her what she wants to hear.

I told her that I wouldn't stay in New York, that I would return to Paris, that way I could be nearer to her and I could come and see her in Brussels regularly. Not every week, but often. Yes, I'd like that, she said. And then I remembered that I don't know how to protect myself.

Immediately I think that I shouldn't have said that to my mother and that maybe I would be better off staying in New York, that way I could call her from time to time on Skype and that would be all. Anyway, we'll see.

My mother says it one more time, I'm not coming back here again.

No. Probably not. I tell her, they'll come and see you instead, my sister and her husband, her niece and her husband, and her grandson whom she fusses over when he lets her.

He's so handsome, she says. Yes, it's true, I reply. And so gentle for a boy, it's surprising. Yes, I say to her, that's true. Sometimes he takes me by the arm and we walk around the block together for a few minutes because I can't manage more than that. And I feel proud and my heart feels full. Yes, I know, maman.

She also adores her granddaughter who has just got married.

Her granddaughter will probably have a child soon, but nobody knows when and no one dares ask her if she plans to. My sister says, I think they're going to wait a little longer, her and her husband. But why wait, there's no time like the present, says my mother, she's not so young anymore, of course she's young but not that young.

Everyone sighs and everyone wishes that my mother would stop bringing up this subject, especially in front of her granddaughter who is very touchy and quick-tempered like her mother. Luckily, she and her husband have just gone off to Asia on their honeymoon. It will be a lovely trip and everyone is very happy for them.

You know, your father and me, we went to Paris for our honeymoon, says my mother, and there were bedbugs in the mattress and the toilet was out in the corridor, and we spent the whole night scratching. Then we came home. But it was still a honeymoon. And the next day we went back to work, we had to work, you know. Yes, maman, I know.

We worked hard all our lives. Yes, maman, I know that, I was there. And you work too. Yes, but not as much. Well, in any case you still work. At the moment I'm not doing much at all. I have nothing in mind, no new ideas. Or too many, I've sometimes thought.

They'll come, my mother replies. That's what you always say. What if this time they don't?

Maman, the nurse is going to dress you now. You put some make-up on, you put some lipstick on even though you can see that it doesn't go with your dressing gown. Oh it's good to have a chat, isn't it. Yes.

My mother says, I'm hungry. They'll be here soon and we'll all eat together. But it's already three o'clock and I'm hungry. In Belgium I eat at half past twelve. Here things are different. Well, why don't you have a bowl of soup while you wait.

The nurse already gave me some soup but it was so watery that I can't feel it. I want them to get back from work, I can't stand all this waiting. Eat some bread then. I can't with this in my mouth, it'll hurt my gums.

Yes, I know. I never should have told her to eat some bread while she was waiting.

Well what about a piece of fruit in the meantime. What, before the meal?

Yes, it's actually better to eat fruit before a meal than after it. I read an article about it.

I don't fancy it.

Well you can't be that hungry then.

She sighs.

The nurse starts to worry.

My mother tries to get up from her armchair.

You see, I still need someone to help me.

Yes, I can see that. But you're already doing better than before. Take a few steps. That'll help you to forget your hunger.

I have no desire to eat even though I'm hungry.

Take a few steps, that'll give you an appetite.

She takes a few steps with the nurse and says a few words to her in French. The nurse smiles and nods though she hasn't understood a word.

My mother leads the nurse towards the dining room, the nurse helps her sit down in her seat.

My sister enters the room and says, ah you're already sitting down. Yes, I was waiting for you all.

Everyone sits down. The food is on the table.

The nurse cuts her meat and vegetables into tiny pieces. My mother can't do it by herself because of her broken shoulder.

Everyone eats enthusiastically except for my mother.

And out of the blue she makes a comment about the way I eat.

My nephew laughs and says, You treat her like a four-year-old child, and everyone laughs.

I don't want to laugh but I do it anyway, to be like everyone else.

My mother says, why are you laughing like that, like an idiot. My child will always be my child. My nephew says, yes of course that's true but you treat her like a child who has never grown up so of course we laugh.

Go on then, laugh at me, says my mother. Laugh, I don't care. Yes, laughing is good, especially because we haven't laughed much since the wedding and especially not about the photo where my mother is smiling during the service. None of us liked that smile.

Anyway laughing does me good and in Harlem I had almost stopped laughing except for sometimes. I had brought her to live in this apartment, in this city she hardly knew. I'd left her first for a wedding then for a dying mother. As for the dying mother, she'd offered to come with me.

I'd said no.

She'd left her apartment, a girlfriend, her job, but every week, sometimes twice a week, I'd tell her, I don't think this is working, we're not getting on. I'd ended up telling her proudly, I don't love you anymore. And she'd said, that's not possible. I know that's not true.

I was proud because I'd finally been able to say something I'd never been able to say before. So I'd said to myself, for once I'm being strong, I'm saying something. I'm saying what I really feel.

I felt spied on, analysed, scrutinised, she had such a keen ear that even when I spoke on the phone and said, you too, she could hear it, she knew that I was saying, I miss you too.

She would come into the bedroom with her eyes black with rage and make me listen to her for hours on end saying that she couldn't put up with it anymore. She was screaming. The dog looked at us one at a time. I stroked her paw and said to her, don't worry, nothing's wrong.

But she was worried. The dog was worried. C. was worried and I was terribly worried, and I was suffocating. I was suffocating more and more every day except when I gave in, when I stopped phoning L., when I stopped finding excuses to leave the house, when I stopped running away from her. No, I was giving in. And the first few days of that were good. And then it became awful again. No, I didn't want to give in, I wanted phone calls and laughter with friends and strangers about everything and nothing. At the wedding, a friend of my sister had come up to my mother and kissed her with such warmth, with such affection even, that my mother had finally smiled.

Then this friend had gone to stand behind my mother and called the photographer over to take a photo of them together. My mother said, I'm not very photogenic anymore, not at all photogenic anymore, even.

Don't be silly, the friend said, of course you are. She'd draped her arms over my mother's scrawny body. The noise of the room was maddening, a mixture of music, shouts, laughs, they were even dancing the hora. You had to shout to be heard.

My mother half opened her mouth for the photo. Immediately I felt sick. A smile held with such effort. Don't smile maman, it's not worth it. But she insisted. Her mouth was held open for a smile and the photographer took her time. My mother waited there, holding herself as upright as she could, her mouth fixed into what might be considered a smile, her face a shade of green, her lips red with too much lipstick. From afar, you might think they were bleeding.

Finally, the photo was taken. I was relieved, and she was too. I'll send it to you, the woman told my mother, with her arms still around her.

That's nice but you don't have to, said my mother. You probably already have a lot more important things to be getting on with. Don't be silly, said my sister's friend.

Maman, it's late, why don't we start heading back.

Yes, it's late, I don't know why but I feel tired. I never used to get tired at weddings.

I know, but it's been a long day. She gives me a look that's almost hostile. That's not a reason. Yes, it is.

But I can't take it anymore. The day started at seven and the photographers arrived at eight and the hairdressers and make-up artists just after that. Luckily you had your hair and make-up done. At least I don't feel ashamed.

I take a sip of wine. Mind you don't spill that. I won't.

Because the stains are impossible to get out. I know. Though sometimes you can.

She waits a bit longer. For a while, she seems less drowsy.

Then she says, but how are we supposed to get home. There's a minibus and a driver over there. That's what they're there for.

Do you think? The anxiety has returned. Yes, I'm sure, but if you want I can go and check. Yes, go and check. She wrings her hands again. I unravel them gently. So she grasps at her clutch bag instead.

And suddenly she asks, what about your dog, where is she. In Paris.

Is someone looking after her? Yes.

When I returned to her side after checking with the minibus driver it was even worse. She couldn't get up. Clara and I helped her up and navigated her across the dance floor and its noises, through groups of dancers and be-

tween tables and thundering screams of joy.

My mother struggled with each step, each time she was more out of breath.

We practically carried her into the minibus and up the stairs of the house and in to her room before undressing her in silence.

Clara and I looked at one another. We knew that this was serious. We said to each other very quietly, this isn't good.

She looked like the living dead, her eyes were transparent, almost lifeless. But they still had a bit of a gleam.

I held her hand as she closed her eyes. I wasn't sure whether she was sleeping but her eyes were closed. She was breathing and gurgling.

The next day she went back to hospital, to A&E.

I was meant to leave that day, to return to my life in New York.

My sister said, go on, there's nothing you can do for her here anyway.

But what if. No, she'll be here when you come back, I'm sure of it. I'm not. Of course she will. She'll be here. Go on, the driver will take you to the airport.

Go back to New York. Go and focus on your work. Go on. Go back.

In New York I couldn't sleep again, night after night.

We'd chosen the apartment for the alcove which separated the two main rooms.

But we'd done it all by email, at a distance, the tenancy agreement, the deposit.

We weren't able to tell that the windows looked out onto the facing wall.

Just a tiny bit of sky.

Sometimes it was blue.

It snowed only once, on a day in November.

C. was delighted.

She felt a bit cold but was delighted.

I got on the plane. And already I felt guilty, I never should have left.

I tried to read but I couldn't. Then I thought, I should prepare myself. But how. I should try and imagine myself without her. But I didn't have any imagination. So I looked out of the window, at the sky, at the clouds. It took so long to get to New York. I thought, we'll never get there. I started to kick the seat in front of mine without realising I was doing it. A woman turned around aggressively and asked me to stop. She couldn't have known, of course. She thought that I was doing it deliberately, that I had no respect for her or her back. I didn't eat or drink. I got up, sat back down. We still hadn't arrived. Nothing to be done. I tried to breathe using the method I'd been taught to use when anxious. But I wasn't even anxious. No. I was just trying to prepare myself for my mother's death.

Then they told us in Spanish and in English that we

should fasten our seatbelts. We were about to land. But I didn't want to land anymore. I wanted to spend the rest of my life on the plane.

But we landed and people started rushing towards the exit, I waited. When everyone had got off I managed to get up. I couldn't feel my legs but I was walking.
The suitcases made their way around the belt. I wasn't paying attention. I waited there like everyone else but I'd forgotten why.

Then suddenly I remembered that I had a suitcase and that I had to take it off the conveyor belt.

But I got mixed up. I took a suitcase that wasn't mine.

Someone came up to me and grabbed the suitcase from my hands, shouting something in Spanish.

I said sorry, graçias. Mucho graçias. I knew that wasn't the right thing to say so I didn't say anything.

I stayed in front of the belt for a while and ended up with my suitcase. It was the only one left so it had to be mine.

In the synagogue, the crowded synagogue, we waited.

The photographers and videographers were already there, standing in my line of sight. I pushed past them. I wanted to see what was about to happen. My cousin was next to me.

Then suddenly the first few notes of the wedding march sounded, we all turned around.

I don't remember the order in which things happened, I know that my brother-in-law walked down the aisle with my niece, his daughter, in a white dress.

And I can't remember the rest. My mother was at the end of the procession, holding onto her grandson's arm. She was walking in a daze. I stroked her cheek as she passed alongside me, then I turned to my cousin and said, I don't think she's got long left. I don't remember how my cousin replied. I think she said, she's very pale, but I'm not sure. I think she lowered her head. You don't talk about death at a wedding. Then a bit later I saw her wipe her eyes and then she said to me, you shouldn't say things like that, and then, you never know, maybe she'll get better. Yes, maybe. But I had trouble believing that. Suddenly my cousin dropped her bag on the floor and we both crouched down to pick up the compact which had broken and to collect the powder that was all over the floor, and her lipstick, a hairbrush, a bit of money. And tissues.

I've forgotten the rest. The broken glass, the exchange of rings. Everything. But there are photos. One day I'll look at them.

On several occasions I pushed past the photographers who were standing on the little podium. But it was no use. I couldn't see a thing. I saw nothing that day except my mother.

And instead of being happy I couldn't stop feeling sick and on top of that I couldn't see a thing.

I'd asked my sister if C. could come with me. She'd said, it's not a good time. I understood and at the same time I didn't. After all, what was the worst that could happen. C. was alone in New York waiting for me. She was alone and didn't know anyone. What's the worst she could have done at a wedding with so many people. Nobody would have noticed her. Or maybe everyone would have. Was she really that different. She didn't speak to me that time in Venice, said my sister. She spoke to me, said her husband. M. could have come, my sister said. When she said that I started to think about M. again. I thought about how close we'd been. I thought about everything that had happened between us. I couldn't remember why it had suddenly come to an end. With C. there was never this closeness except on Facebook and a little while after that. A little while after that, yes, but not in the same way. That's normal though because they're different people and because C. was so young. So it was different. I can't deny it. It was an entirely different thing. Afterwards, bit by bit, something seemed lost. Something else took its place. Then everything came to a halt. Luckily C. couldn't read my mind from a distance. I said to myself, it's lucky she didn't come this time after all.

My sister said, and L. could have come, she's like family.

But not C. I understand, I said, and then I'd felt angry at myself for understanding my sister's point of view. My sister wanted things to go well. And all the people that were invited belonged, but not C.

I tried to dance a bit to be like everyone else. That's what I'd always done at weddings, especially when I was young and my father was still alive.

My sister told the men, the boys, that they should put me on a chair which they'd raise up and lower several times.

Then I went back to sit near my mother. She was staring into space. And her dress was lopsided because of her broken shoulder.

I don't even think she had the strength to be happy about the wedding and a grandmother should be happy. What was she thinking about. About everything that was hurting her, probably. From time to time she wrung her hands. I couldn't stand that.

Before that she'd loved to dance, at weddings and elsewhere, on holiday in Italy and other places besides, and she'd danced well.

In New York C. wrote a few emails, including one to our landlord who was a young woman. Later on we met her along with her mother, a very elegant woman in a hat. C. wrote that we were still having a few problems with the apartment and that she'd just seen a mouse run along the corridor into the living room. She wrote that it was a tiny mouse but that it was a mouse nonetheless and she wasn't used to mice and probably never would be but that if she had to get used to them she would try. Still, she hoped she wouldn't see any others.

She knew that if there was one mouse there would soon be more, so even if she had to she wouldn't get used to them. When she was little she'd read a book about destitute people living in Harlem who were attacked by rats and she thought that if there were mice there might one day be rats too. She'd seen the mouse go into a hole near the radiator and she'd managed to seal it up. But there were other holes and she couldn't spend her whole life sealing them up.

She'd also written that the washing machine no longer worked properly and at the end of the cycle there was still water in the bottom and that this wasn't normal.

But what else had C. done alone in New York. I phoned her and she said, you sound awful. Really. I hadn't realised. In the end it was a good thing that she hadn't come because at the dinner before the wedding I'd laughed with a young boy who made me laugh. That's all.

She wouldn't have liked that. She would have said, that's called flirting. But for me it was nothing, just a desire to laugh. A need to laugh in the face of oncoming disaster. Like laughing at an erupting volcano. Everyone seemed surprised that I was laughing so much and everyone seemed surprised by my good mood. In spite of this, C.

had told me over the phone, you sound awful. She had sensed from afar what was beneath this laugh. But luckily she hadn't heard the laugh itself or else she would have been hurt. Now I say hurt but at the time I would have said jealous, jealous for no reason. As though I didn't have the right to laugh a little.

There was good wine and good food and an amusing young boy next to me and so I laughed, I teased him a bit and we had a good laugh. It'd been a long time since I'd laughed like that, so long that I'd forgotten that it was even possible to laugh like that.

In New York I had to be careful when I laughed. I still laughed sometimes but a lot less than usual. And I missed it and I went into that dark place where only going out into the street to call my friends could calm me down.

And I couldn't hear well because of the noise but I still laughed and felt good.

I phoned my friends in Paris and I felt good.

Someone had said to my sister, I never knew your sister was like that, so full of laughter.

She is, my sister had replied, why wouldn't she be?

But my laughter didn't last long. By the next day I wasn't laughing at all.

My sister was right in saying it wasn't a good time for C. to come, I thought. My sister is often right. And this time she was especially right, and deep down I'd known she was right because I hadn't argued with her when she said that it wasn't a good time for C. to come. Not to her daughter's wedding in any case. I hadn't insisted and deep down I was happy even though I felt angry at myself. Yes, I was angry at myself but I told myself, get over it. Anyway, I was certain C. wouldn't have enjoyed it, and she was a shy person, but that's not the reason.

By ten in the morning on the day of the wedding, everyone had arrived.

There was a huge crowd in the house. Photographers, hairdressers, make-up artists, everyone was there and everyone was bustling around. Everything was photographed, every second of life.

The smallest gesture, smile, movement on the stairs. Or elsewhere. Everything was photographed and everyone had to smile at all times.

My niece was at the top of the stairs. Her wedding dress was being arranged.

Her dress was magnificent, my niece was magnificent and smiling.

Clara placed the veil on her head. Then she took one pose and then another.

And everything, absolutely everything, was photographed.

After a little while I said, I'm starting to get sick of these photographers. My niece replied, it's only just begun. A bit drily, maybe, or with a little bit of humour and a bit of distance. No, without any distance. Definitely without any distance. But probably with some humour. Actually, I have no idea. What was I doing there. I'd been against this all my life. Even so, I had been to a great number of weddings especially when I was young and every time I'd tried to put on a brave face and seem carefree and young for my father. I don't know whether he knew it at that time, that I was an odd one, but I could tell that he hoped that one day it'd be my turn.

If I was anti-marriage why had I been at so many weddings which were always such a palaver to attend because you had to get dressed up in order to be there and when I dressed up I was less visible and so people didn't whisper

to each other, that one over there isn't married yet. To belong, probably, but I still didn't belong. No, not at all. And I was anti-marriage. But probably not enough not to go. This time it was my niece's wedding and thanks to my sister I had a niece and I belonged a bit. I belonged but I felt even more alone. More alone than ever.

But I had a niece and a nephew and I loved them. So I felt less alone.

And so deep down it didn't really matter if one of them got married except that for them it did and for lots of other people too.

It didn't change anything and I loved them and that's all that mattered.

For C. it would have been even worse. She didn't even have a niece. And my niece wasn't her niece. She could have become her niece but everyone pretended C. didn't exist.

But she did exist, she was waiting for me in New York and she had a very strong presence. Or too real a presence, too much in general. Beautiful but in a strange way. Too severe, probably. Sometimes gentle, sometimes short-tempered, sometimes shy. She wouldn't have been able to stand this wedding. It wasn't her kind of fun. She would have shut herself in a corner for the whole day so everyone would have seen that she was in a corner not smiling. She wasn't like me, she wouldn't have tried to belong. She would have just shut down. She would have given a bad atmosphere to a day where everything had been designed to create joy. My sister would have been embarrassed. My brother-in-law would have said it's not a big deal but everyone would have noticed and it might have even cast a shadow over the day.

Yet when she'd met my niece a year earlier, when my loved-up niece and her fiancé had come to visit for a week around Christmas and we'd gone out to an Italian restaurant, things seemed to have gone smoothly. C. was smiling and listening attentively to what was being said, as usual. I'd never met a listener like C. before. At the beginning I liked it. And when I'd said to her, among many other things, I feel like an octopus has got me in its tentacles and won't let me go (I'd said octopus because we were in Greece, otherwise I probably would have said something else), she'd listened to me attentively before saying, well, let's get this octopus off you, one arm at a time, and you'll be saved.

MY MOTHER LAUGHS

She'd wanted to save me. I could feel it. Yes, that's what she'd wanted from the start and even at the end.

My niece had said she's sweet but isn't she a bit young for you.

Probably. I'd shrugged. The restaurant was very dark. We'd had a lot to drink. I didn't tell C. what my niece had said, I knew exactly what she would have said, I'm not that young and what does it matter anyway.

I remember that evening being a good one even though we'd already started to argue by that point, all because L. had phoned me a few times.

We'd started to argue and it was the first time. In fact it was the second but I'd already forgotten the first. I hadn't taken that argument seriously. I should have.

That first time had been the first in a long series of arguments.

And in that beginning you could already find the end.

All that brought us to where we ended up. But I hadn't understood, I hadn't seen anything coming because nothing like this had never happened to me before.

I should have been cautious but I lacked caution.

I should have sensed that I should end it there, after the first argument, that I would never be able to put up with the ones to come. I've always hated arguments, I'm no good at them and especially not with C. who was so persuasive. Yes, she was so persuasive that I thought she must be right and gave in. I'd never experienced that before. I'd never lived in fear of the next argument. I'd often felt like there was no room to breathe. But never before had I felt constantly watched.

I even had to watch my laugh. Not every kind of laugh, but one in particular, and it could be with someone I knew or a stranger, like a waiter, for example, or someone else, a light meaningless laugh, one that was in the moment and never went any further.

Later on C. also met my nephew, in New York again but long after the wedding. When I'd asked him whether he thought she was too young he said, young people are better, and I felt sick. I thought about myself, not C. I knew that meant that he thought that I wasn't young and so I wasn't better.

Now I'm tossing and turning in my Harlem bed and I realise that I can feel the octopus's tentacles around me again, that they're still there.

I open one eye. I recognise the bedroom in Harlem.

C. is here, next to me. For better or for worse. She's asleep.

Her little black eyes are closed. She opens them. Smiles. Says hello in Greek and then a tender word. I breathe. I think to myself it's going to be a good day. Not like yesterday or the day before that.

Yes, the sleepless nights had begun again.

But she always ended up getting to sleep.

If ever I managed to get to sleep I would wake up very

soon afterwards with my eyes full of tears.

Then in the middle of the day I would go and place myself proudly in front of her and say, look, this isn't working. I was proud because I was finally managing to say something.

Her heavy eyes were on me again, flickering between anger and pain.

I had almost stopped eating. I got cramps and felt sick.
She watched me suspiciously.
Packages kept arriving. Presents for me.
I accepted them joylessly.

We ended up spending nearly the whole night watching films on Netflix, on our plasma screen.

Those were the times we felt good together.

Then she would put on some gentle music which was meant to soothe me and put me to sleep but it never worked.
Why?
I don't know.
That's not true.
Yes it is.

Yes, there were times when we were happy together. Yes, happy. Quite simply happy. Sometimes after awful arguments.

We were both exhausted so we felt much better and let the argument come to its end.
Sometimes she would sleep on top of me and these strange sobs would suddenly overwhelm her. Rasping, childlike sobs. She's crying, she's coming. She's crying or she's coming. Maybe both at the same time. I'd never heard anything like it.

Sometimes I would react.
Sometimes I would stay still.
Death meat, she would say in English. Yes, dead meat.
But we knew we were happy.

My sister had said, go. So I went. I'd told C. a bit about the wedding but not too much. She'd listened, too much. Before, I'd liked that. Now I liked it less. Especially when it was stories of a wedding she'd not been invited to.

And the rest. I hadn't told her I'd laughed with a young boy. No, I'd made sure not to tell her that.

In fact I'd hardly told her anything about the wedding and especially not that I'd laughed or that at the synagogue the men sat on one side and the women sat on the other or that there had been so many people there. Or that my niece hadn't stopped smiling or that my sister had worn a beautiful dress. No, none of that. I'd just told her about my mother and that I'd felt sick, terribly sick. C. said, maybe your mother's dying, just like she'd said when my mother had gone into A&E. I'd wanted to tell her that's not what you say but I knew that it was just something to say and especially for C., who knew about these things, so I didn't say anything at all.

But I wanted to be alone. I didn't want to be listened to so intently or watched or even scrutinised. She saw everything even when there was nothing to see. She heard everything even when there was nothing much to hear. She suffered from this nothing. I did too.

It was stifling. I couldn't take it anymore. I knew that she was suffering and I couldn't take it.

And she never stopped asking me, why can't you sleep.

One day someone mistook her for my daughter at the

supermarket. And C. had smiled. She'd said, age doesn't matter. Does it matter to you? I was lying when I'd said no. And when I'd met her at the train station in London for the first time I'd got a shock, she looked about 17. She'd said nothing. I said to myself, I'm mad and then, but who cares.

Her walk had something of a 17-year-old girl, even though she was thirty. She laughed. Whenever she suddenly broke her silence with a laugh, like a 17-year-old girl, I thought to myself again, who cares.

That was how she walked and laughed, but the way she watched me was heavy and dark.

I'd arrived in London with a suitcase stuffed full of books, very serious books.

I'd just about flicked through a couple of them on the train. That was it. I never read them. It hadn't felt like the right time. The right time had never come. And I hadn't bothered to put them out at the bus stop for someone else to read either. That's what I'd got into the habit of doing with the books that I'd read. And the books would always disappear. One day I thought I should stand across the road from the bus stop to see who was taking the books, to see who was interested in my kind of books, but I never did it.

Anyway, that's the reason I'm not weighed down with books and that every time I buy more I can always find somewhere to put them in my apartment in Paris.

In London we ate, we drank, I talked without stopping, we kissed, we loved each other. Yes, we loved each other, we'd already loved each other for so long, we'd loved each other before we'd even met, we'd loved each other as soon as we'd started writing to each other and maybe we should have continued to love each other like that. Yes, at that time we were madly in love.

We loved each other over email, over texts, over Facebook. She sent me songs, sometimes in Greek sometimes not, poems in Greek sometimes not, sometimes even in English or French, or any other language. I listened to the songs. I read the poems. My heart was beating. Life was beginning again.

But not anymore. Now it feels like the end of life.

We could no longer breathe.

Luckily there was the dog.

It was later on that she hit me, in New York, in the apartment I'd rented and in which she'd made me a home. A home with everything you might need inside it, even my special sugar cubes.

It was later on that I left the apartment with a black eye.

Later on that she rammed the edge of the table into my stomach.

She was suffering so badly and was so angry that she rammed the edge of the table into my stomach at least 15 times. I didn't count them but I think it must have been at least 15 times, a few minutes before she sent me out to the shop to buy cigarettes. I let it happen and so no, I didn't count. I began to realise that I should just wait for it to finish. She was suffering, she was so wounded that she couldn't stop herself from doing it. But it was only later, much later, that I noticed her wound. Too late. I could only see the rage and her little dark black eyes. Eyes without pupils, or maybe the opposite.

I couldn't feel a thing but I thought, I have to defend myself.

So when she hit me I thought, I have to hit her too, but they weren't real punches. I wasn't sure how to go about it but I managed. I thought to myself, hit her back. You have to hit her back. So I did. I don't know if I regret it and I don't know why I thought, hit her back.

After she'd hit me in the eye she'd wanted to take care of me.

I didn't want her to.

She came over to me with a wet flannel. I didn't want it.

Her rage had come back and I was a bit scared. I started holding my forearms against my body with my fists clenched like I'd seen in boxing matches.

The day before or maybe on a different day she'd said to me, you're not leaving this room until you respond. I no longer remember what I was meant to be responding to. I was feeling proud of my silence and my only thought was, what happens if I need to pee. She was standing in front of the door watching me. Her face was expressionless.

I had the feeling that she was going to stand in front of the door for ever.

Then afterwards she said that it'd just been a turn of phrase.

That was a few days before she hit me.

I'd told her, you're really getting on my nerves, going on about the way I open or close my laptop, something she couldn't stand. So I told her. It wasn't nice and she wasn't going to put up with it and I can understand that. So then there were blows, pain, her own pain, a wide-open wound. But the blows in the end weren't really that violent.

Before that my sister had rented a house near Mexico where my mother could breathe more easily thanks to the low altitude. Of course she didn't want C. But she wanted me to come. I'd said, I can't.

You could at least try and tell her that you need to be close to your mother right now. I can't.

My sister said, then I'll call myself to tell her your mother needs you. No, don't do that.

Things had got so bad that I didn't dare do anything and I decided it was better for me to just stay there.

But I'd wanted to go. I'd wanted to go to be far away from C. and to breathe but I never managed to tell her that. I wanted to go and see my mother and my sister.

So I got angry at myself and at C. too.

On Christmas Day I thought, I'm going to make an effort, I'll bring home a Christmas tree. I brought home a tree that I'd found on the street and took it upstairs. But we couldn't work out where to put it or how to get it to stand up so she went out to buy something to put it in and even bought a string of little multi-coloured lights. They were the worst of all, the little lights in the middle of our silence.

And it all ended badly.

Two days later I left her there with the dog, the tree and the lights, there in the dark apartment. It was my best friend in New York who came to pick me up. I'd managed to pack my bags behind her back. Or if she'd seen them she hadn't said anything. But I don't think she had because she spent all day in the bedroom without moving and my bags were in the little study where I never worked.

The taxi driver drove so quickly that me and my friend kept bashing into each other. I told him thank you. He said, you don't need to thank me, then he said, she's not going to kill herself is she.

I was scared, I thought about it, I said no. Because of the dog. She loves that dog too much and the dog loves her.

I immediately went to join my mother and sister in the rented house. It was after the hitting and straight away my mother picked up on something. She said, your face looks deformed but I could be wrong because my vision is blurred. I said, you're probably right.

My sister looked at me with pity and my brother-in-law said, it'll soon heal.

And all of a sudden my sister acknowledged C.'s existence because of her pity for me.

And she said, but how is it possible. I shrugged and said, we had good times. Times where I felt alive.

Times when I thought that everything could be fixed, even my body's rotten tissue.

My sister snapped back, your tissue isn't rotten, you're just fragile, that's all.

Anyway, in Milan someone read my palm and he told me that I should be looking out for you. Really? I was stunned. Did he really say that? Yes. Anyway, I often worry about you. You should be more careful. But I am careful and I take my medicine every day. No, you're not careful enough and it scares me. You're always off gallivanting, taking planes goodness knows where when you know perfectly well that jetlag doesn't agree with you. You'd be better off taking it easy. And worrying less. You worry too much. No, I don't. Yes you do, I can see it in your eyes. But you worry a lot too. Yes, sometimes, but not like you. When you worry it escalates, it becomes serious and dangerous for you. And I'm not often with you and when I am and I say something you don't listen. You tell me it's nothing, that it'll pass. And it has always passed, it's true.

Up until now it's always passed. But who knows.

I've read up about your illness and people often throw themselves out of windows because of it. Not me. No, not up till now. But you get ill too often, I can't bear it.

Well me neither but I know that it always passes and that's what I tell myself every day. That's just how it is. I've got it and there's nothing I can do about it.

But it shouldn't be this way.

But it's not my fault.

No it isn't really but you don't protect yourself enough. Just look at yourself with that black eye. You won't be seeing her again, I hope. I really don't understand how it came to this.

Me neither.

I told you I never liked her. My brother-in-law interjects, leave her alone, she's your sister. That's the point, my sister replies.

I know you never liked her but she wanted to help me through my illness and one day she even said to me, I've made a home for you, but I hadn't even noticed. And she was born prematurely and her mother died when she was young. What's that got to do with anything? I don't know if it does. We spent a lot of time talking. Yes, you'll talk to anyone and then they end up hitting you.

But this is the first time. No one's ever hit me before.

Yes, but people have hurt you before. Who? These girls, they've hurt you. That's not true. Not all of them, no. Not all but a lot of them, she says.

No, not a lot of them. Why are you saying that?

I told my sister that I'd said you're really getting on my nerves. She said, that's no reason to hit you and look at you, you need a haircut, look at your hair, it's lost all its shape. There are good hairdressers here, you know.

My mother overheard this. She said, go on. It'll take your mind off things.

No, I said to my sister out of my mother's earshot. A haircut will make my black eye even more obvious.

I'll go and buy you some giant sunglasses to hide it but you'll still be able to see it in profile. She must have hit you really hard. Not really. And anyway I put my fists in front of my face and thought to myself I'll hit her back. You, hit someone? That'll be the day.

Maybe she had hit me hard but I hadn't felt a thing.

That day all I could see was her rage. But now I can also feel her pain.

C. had sent me out to buy cigarettes. I had my mobile with me and behind her back I called my best friend, H. Yes, he'd said, I'm on my way.

When I returned home I threw the cigarettes in her face. I'd seen people do that in films so that's what I did. But it was phoney. She knew it but she didn't say anything.

H. arrived almost immediately. He looked pale. C. looked pale. I looked pale.

H. exchanged a few words with C. in a very gentle voice. I can't remember what he said.

He picked up my bags and we went out. She didn't follow. Nor did the dog.

A few days later C. went back to London with the dog. She moved into an attic in Zone 3. I only found this out later on.

Someone had invited her to stay. She'd left a few boxes in the Harlem apartment. They contained all her belongings, except the things she'd left in Paris for later. I had to deal with them. I had to send them to England. She'd sent

me an email with the address. I'd never heard of the area.

We spent New Year's Day in the house my sister had rented. We drank champagne. The house had a swimming pool but my mother could only look at it from afar.

She was too weak and the nurse was still with her. She asked me how things were going in New York. Good, I said.

It must be nice there and I'm happy you're teaching at a university, my daughter who never even studied. Aren't you pleased? I don't know. But you will carry on, won't you?

I don't know. You don't know? I don't know. You always say you don't know.

But what are your students and your apartment like? Nice.

It has a long corridor. You love long corridors, you always put them in your films. Yes, and at the end of the corridor there are two bedrooms, one smaller than the other. On the left-hand side there are two doors, one leading to the kitchen, the other to a light blue bathroom with a window.

In the kitchen, there's everything you need.

A fridge.

A gas cooker with an oven.

A microwave.

A big sink. A dishwasher.

A washing machine.

On the other side of the corridor there are two other rooms but they don't have doors.

Opposite the kitchen is a dining room.

With a black table. Six black chairs. A black sideboard.

My mother said, it's good to have a washing machine and a microwave. Yes. It's good. But why is all the furniture black? Please tell me you have a cleaning lady at least? Yes, sometimes, but she speaks Spanish. You must get a cleaning lady in at least once a week. Especially with your mess. Yes.

In the beginning I'd walked around in a strange state, though maybe it was my default state. I was up for anything, for giving as well as receiving. After that she continued to give but I could no longer see it except on occasion.

But I didn't want to give anything anymore, except for maybe an ugly sofa, the cheapest one I could find on the street. Stingy, cheap, that's what she'd written to me months later. Yes and no. Probably, yes, my only defence.

That's what I think now, anyway. I make excuses for myself.

But I was waging a war, an underground, cold war. I shouldn't have.

Even now I can't imagine what I could or should have done. If we were to start over, I would probably do the same again but differently.

I'd passed the sofa on the street several times. It was there on the pavement in front of the shop window. I'd even tried it out. I liked it, I liked it more and more every time I passed it.

I'd ended up saying, come and have a look at this sofa. I'd said, the shop is horrible and so is most of the furniture but this sofa has a certain something, I didn't know what but it's really not bad, what do you think.

Her little brown eyes had darted around before landing on the sofa. Yes, she didn't think it was bad either, all things considered.

We bought it.

It was delivered.

We put it in the empty room.

We were happy.

We both liked this sofa.

Then she ordered a whole bunch of things.

We put these things around the sofa it so that it was less visible, probably.

At the supermarket, the one where someone had mistaken her for my daughter, we couldn't find any sugar cubes. And I can only drink my coffee if I had a sugar cube. I would put a sugar cube between my teeth and then drink the coffee. I think my three aunts must have done the same in their day.

One day the doorbell rang, it was a day when I could hear.

I got up, I went to open the door.

There was a courier with a small package.

I opened it with a kind of fake enthusiasm.

It was sugar cubes.

There were still some left when I came back and she had

already left and I was very happy. I like to drink coffee with a sugar cube on my tongue or between my teeth.

That's the way I drink it. I don't like to put sugar in the actual coffee.

There were also chocolate-coated nuts, some powder for hot chocolate. She had a sweet tooth.

And today in Paris I saw Danone rice puddings and Greek yoghurt. I nearly bought them.

I used to buy her those kind of things and also crème caramels. We'd pass them between our mouths.

At the beginning it'd been like a cataclysm with burning flames and exaltation.

Words, the same words repeated over and over again, I'd even become acquainted with the words of love in a dead language.

I talked so much. I shouldn't have.

Yes, I was starting to live again.

I stopped seeing my mother die.

I stopped not living.

There was life in me.

A whole life.

A full life.

My mother sighs. It's in the morning that I feel bad, that I feel the worst. After that I loosen up a bit, wouldn't you say? She keeps her eyes closed during her Mexican breakfast. Only opens them when I talk. As soon as I stop she closes them again. Tell me something. You must have something to tell me.

But what? Whatever you want, what you're up to right now, tell me. Anything.

OK, I'll try. But nothing, absolutely nothing, comes to mind. What do you want me to tell you. Anything, it's all interesting to me.

Tell me about your class in New York. Oh no, anything but that. There's nothing to say. I teach there three hours a week, that's all. I have fourteen students, that's it.

They come from all over the world. There you go.
I tried to find something to say about the year which had just come to an end and which had been horrible. Horrible nearly all the time. With shouting, interminable silences, blows, insomnia, diarrhoea, mice, exterminators, falls, twisted ankles, bloody knees, cold sweats, hot sweats. I wasn't going to tell her all of that. Or the rest.

Coffee in bed. Pasta in bed. Camomile tea. Half-hearted

kisses. Not even the cold or the heat or this funny climate. Or the morning with the dog. Anyway, my mother has never liked small dogs, she wouldn't have liked C.'s dog either. She wouldn't have felt sorry for it when it was cold and it was cold in New York and the dog barked.

Yes it was cold when we walked along FDR Drive and along the river.

The wind was blowing at a hundred miles an hour, maybe less but it was very strong.

The dog was shivering. So were we.

She barked whenever she saw another dog. Why.

Fear, probably. You can't do much about that.

In the evening we hardly ever made it as far as the river. We went onto the grassy central strip in the middle of Broadway, it wasn't as far. But cars zoomed past on either side and there were poor people who sat there for most of the day. We would walk up and down with her until finally she would sit down with dignity and push out a little poo. Then we'd rush back home.

Sometimes it took her a long time, a ridiculously long time. We would have liked to rush her but she had her own rhythm, she would sit down when it was the right time, her time. It took a lot of back and forth on this little strip of grass, lined with benches and poor people.

Sometimes there was nothing we could do about it, she didn't want to sit down.

Now's your time, we'd tell her, we're not going out again today, but she didn't care.

And if she saw someone or a dog from afar, she would bark. Stop. But she would bark. Sometimes it annoyed me, sometimes I let her go for it. I told myself, she needs to bark.

Especially since we'd started muzzling her every time we left the apartment. And it broke our hearts to muzzle her. But nothing got past our Asian neighbour. He must have been on edge what with his newborn and his depressed wife. After a few weeks I saw him in the street and asked him if everything was better. Yes, he could no longer hear the dog but there was now water coming through the ceiling of his bathroom, I must have left the tap running one time and let the water overflow. I told him that I hadn't. But he was right.

After a few weeks we decided to stop muzzling her, we said to each other that she must have got used to her new environment by now. So we left the apartment, closing the door behind us, and we stood listening at the door for a long time. But nothing. She walked around a bit, then she must have settled down on the bed. We were relieved. At least one problem had been solved.

Luckily for her we rarely went out and never for long. We went to the supermarket or the Mexican restaurant on the corner where we were always alone with the giant television which always seemed to be on at full volume and we could talk about that, about the noise that was unbearable. I even tried to talk to the waitress about it who didn't speak a word of English.

So I put my hands over my ears to try and explain to her, I turned an imaginary volume dial with my fingers to communicate the idea of lowering the volume, she lowered it a little, too little. Sometimes there was a tired-looking man who drank beer after beer at the bar, he probably needed some noise. It probably made him happy. Then one day the restaurant suddenly closed down.

What a shame. I liked the place, it was our local restaurant. I've always liked my local restaurant, in Paris, in Brussels, in Harlem, always.

In Mexico there was no local restaurant or even a place that sold cigarettes or newspapers. Everything was far away. You had to have a car and I've never passed my driving test. I once said to C., you should learn, then we can take a road trip across America. She agreed but never did it.

Next to the local restaurant there was an infamous bodega where I bought cigarettes. I haggled the price because someone told me I had to so that's what I did and the price got lower every time.

The cigarettes were hidden somewhere in the back and the boss would send his nephew to get them. He would shout, Elias! Yellow was the name of my preferred brand. The boss made hundreds of big gestures to communicate the fact that these cigarettes weren't, let's say, strictly legal, that they were illegal. I wondered where he'd got them but it remained a mystery.

Of course the dog wasn't allowed into this dive so I left her in front of the shop with the leash which pulled on my arm. Later on I saw a dog in there so I brought her in with me and the boss who had stuck some Suras on a wooden noticeboard to his left said nothing. But I knew that for people who read the Qur'an my dog would be considered impure.

No, there was nothing that could be said to a mother.

I looked for something but found nothing. So I said, I don't like New York anymore, even with its blue winter sky. You don't like New York anymore, but you've always loved New York. Not anymore. New York has changed or maybe it's me. Maybe I'm no longer cut out for New York. My mother said, I went to New York once. We arrived there in a car from Canada. With dad and your uncle and aunt.

When we passed through Harlem your uncle locked the windows. He said, this area is very dangerous for white people. And now that's where you live. But maman, it's not like that anymore, it's not dangerous at all now. And when I've been away and I arrive home with my suitcases there's always someone from my building who helps me and sometimes he or she will say, it's for God that I'm doing this. And I smile and I say but in the meantime you're doing it for me too.

Are they really that religious there? I don't know but I think that in my building they are.

You know, I'm not very religious but still a little bit. I can sense something up in the sky but I don't know what it is. Sometimes I wonder. What about you? Me? No. I wish I was though.

Maybe I'd feel at peace.

Yes, my father was very much at peace, he was terribly religious. He was a wonderful, very gentle man, probably because of his belief, but even he disappeared along with the others.

It's such a shame but above all it's sad. I would have liked you to get to know them both. They were very different but they got on well despite their differences, it was an arranged marriage but they got on, two people couldn't have got on any better than they did. You know, at least they had that, those years of harmony before they vanished.

He had a wonderful voice and she had dainty hands and you should have seen how she painted. Deep down they were both artists so you do have someone to take after.

Afterwards I returned for a short while to Paris and to Brussels. With my black eye and my sunglasses.
 Without foundation because I always put it on badly.
 I could see them looking at me at the border.
 So I hid my nose with a finger.

I came home to my apartment, with the rug in the living room, the fake Persian rug which I'd bought from a shopkeeper as if it was a real Persian rug and I'd paid a lot for it, for this fake Persian rug but I didn't care. I wanted this rug and that was that.
 And I'm still glad I bought this rug and anyway it's beautiful even if it is a fake. I look at it and I say to myself, I really like this rug. It's very rare that I buy something for myself so when it happens I'm very happy, even if I'm buying something fake.

In Paris I felt alone. Nobody listened to me or watched me.
 I felt alone but good.
 Nobody asked me, why aren't you sleeping.
 Nobody listened in on my calls.
 Nobody watched or even looked at me.

But still I thought to myself, I should remember that sometimes we were happy. And that counts for something.
 And that sometimes light reflected across the walls.
 I don't know how, but it did and it made us feel good.

Three times I'd told her, I feel happy with you. Once in the little bedroom on the ground floor on one of the Greek islands. The other time I can't remember but I know it happened and the third time was on the terrace of the

Mexican restaurant in Harlem where we both drank cocktails. After that I got ill but it didn't matter. It was the day she'd arrived, or thereabouts. It was hot. They let us smoke on this terrace, no one looked at us, no one made any remarks, yes, we were happy.

After that it was never the same again and I went to buy the ugliest furniture on Broadway and it was no coincidence.

I made a home for you, that's what she said to me one day and it was true and I hadn't even noticed it.

Yes, all the delivery men that had rung at the door one after the other were delivering things to make me a home but when I heard the doorbell I'd just say, not again.

She was bleeding and I hadn't even noticed. I hadn't seen a thing. Not even that her beautiful face had become dark and tragic. Not even that her pupils were disappearing into her eyes. I couldn't see anything anymore. I couldn't even turn to look at her. Not even that.

I went to Brussels for work and stayed in the big, empty apartment belonging to my mother.

Nobody was there groaning. Nobody was at the hospital. Nobody was making a list. There was no carer. There was just me, watching TV. It was very cold but the kids from the ground floor were still playing in the garden.

I thought to myself, I better not make a mess. One day she'll be back. And the mess will be the first thing she sees.

So I didn't make one and when I left I closed the door firmly and locked it with the key.

The key had to be turned four times in the lock and that's what I did.

It never used to be that way, one time used to be enough, but after the burglary in which all the jewellery my father had given my mother had been stolen we had to have reinforced doors fitted. And the key had to be turned four times in the lock for the insurance company to replace things if ever anything else happened.

Everyone kept saying, Brussels has changed, now there are murders, burglaries, people attacked without warning in the street, you must get your door reinforced. I did everything I was supposed to and didn't harm anyone. Even when I think about it carefully, I don't see what harm I could have done. And anyway I was all alone and I had already done enough harm. This was harm enough and it was for ever.

In Harlem, I often forgot to lock the door and nothing ever happened.

Then I got on another plane. My eye was less black and my nose was straighter.

When I returned to Harlem, exhausted and overloaded with bags, I realised I'd dropped my mother's keys somewhere on the street, I'd been told, whatever you do don't lose them, and I'd said, it's only when someone tells me not to lose something that I lose it, and that's what had happened, they were lost. When I got home I left my bags in the corridor where the light was still on, the first thing I saw was C.'s pile of boxes and a bag which would soon be collected and when I went into the kitchen I saw that the red light on the electric mouse trap was on. We'd already put a lot of effort into fighting these mice. We'd even had a man round with a roll of orange metallic tape. He'd told us plainly, they'll eat it and die. I'd gagged a bit, was that really what we had to do. He was used to it, it didn't bother him at all anymore, we'd even sealed up a few holes but they were still here.

I told myself, I'll sort it out tomorrow, and the next day I took the box and I slid the dead, shrivelled up mouse into a plastic bag and went downstairs to throw it away.

I'll think about the boxes tomorrow.

And the next day the boxes were gone.

There weren't even that many boxes but the apartment seemed empty without them.

I thought, emptiness is better anyway.

Even though there weren't even that many they still had a very strong presence.

I like this silence, even though I'd talked so much at the start. I like this silence and no one is here to reproach me for it.

At the beginning, I'd talked. An incessant stream of words.

I'd said everything and nothing and quickly, I had to tell her about all the years that separated us. I probably shouldn't have. But I only decided that later, much later, when everything started to break down because of all those years and the old flames, those stories from the past which had never had closure.

I'd spoken quickly. She'd said nothing. She'd listened with awful concentration.

No one had ever listened to me like that before.

Later, much later, I learned about her, I listened to her telling me that she'd been born too early, about how she'd been too small, weighing only two kilograms, born just after her twin sister. They'd put her in an incubator where her father had noticed her little brown eyes that kept darting around, looking at everything, promising eyes. Her father already loved her, he never stopped loving her, her mother stopped when everything stopped.

They had three little girls. The father and the mother had done everything they could for their three little girls, I think. Especially the mother who wanted a better life for her girls. So she made these girls study and more, much more. She was strict and well respected from what I can tell. I never met her, or her father or her sisters for that matter. I think I once saw her stepmother on Skype, yes I'm pretty sure of it, a stepmother of around my age, full of life. That's all I remember about this stepmother. The only other mother of that kind I know is my sister's mother-in-law. I remember her very well. She died very young too, like C.'s mother. But C.'s mother died much younger than that, even. So young that she never got to see the three little girls she'd placed so much hope in grow up, the girls for whom she'd wanted a better life than her own, she never saw what became of them after her death. She never found out if they'd suffered or how they'd managed to pull through, whether they'd pulled through with ease or difficulty. She never knew that C. had written a thesis and that she was a writer and that she also played the saxophone. Her mother was dead and it was for ever and of course it's not fair to die so young because you are a woman, dying of a woman's illness. Or for any other reason. But there's nothing to be done, she's dead. Of course you get one day closer to death every day, but even so, definitive death when you're so young just isn't fair. Especially when you have a husband and three little girls but even if you don't it wouldn't be fair, especially when you haven't made the choice and even if you have, that's because a life where you get one day closer to death every day is unliveable and horrible, as it was for L.'s brother who I loved so much. He was like a little brother to me, even though he was nearly six and a half feet tall.

Life had become unliveable for him. But he had everything, including two sisters. And he wrote, he'd written, until the end. When he'd first started writing he'd asked me to read it and I'd said, you're a writer. A real writer. But he only got the chance to write and rewrite one beautiful book. Then it was the end.

He lived through hell and couldn't wait any longer. But I don't really want to think about it. It happened a long time ago though it feels like yesterday and we had great times together. We drank cocktails on café terraces. We talked about everything including the film we'd just been to see.

His death had been horrible for everyone who knew him and my father, who was still alive at the time, had said to his sister, he's happy now, he's in peace, it's you and your sister and your parents and all those who loved him who will suffer now, and it was true but it wasn't really much of a consolation. And at the funeral there were lots of young people and having all these young people around was awful because it was a reminder that he'd been young too, and the fact that it was sunny that day made it even worse. A sun out of season, not at the right time, just like his death.

L. had fainted at the airport when she'd heard there was nothing more that could be done for her brother and that he was gone for ever. She'd fainted when she saw her sister shake her head. She knew from this gesture that there was nothing more they could do. We had a friend with us, a friend who unfortunately I no longer see, unfortunately because I still love this friend but he probably doesn't feel

the same, otherwise we'd still see each other.

But he was the one who drove us to Charles de Gaulle airport and later drove me to Brussels when my father died. At that time he was still my friend, a friend who I thought of deep down as my brother, my big brother because we had so much in common.

We still do but he doesn't want to or can no longer be my friend, in any case he's not able to be close to me and it makes me feel sick when I think about it. Luckily I don't think about it often otherwise I would feel sick all the time and I already feel sick fairly often and sometimes I feel like I've had enough of feeling sick so often so I avoid thinking about lots of things but it doesn't make any difference because I still feel sick so I lie down and sleep. I spend a lot of my life asleep.

Sometimes I spend nearly all day asleep but it's not a problem because I really like my bed, especially the one in Paris and also the one in Brussels, the one in New York a bit less because it's too soft and makes my back ache. Thankfully one of my students cut up some wooden planks the size of my mattress because after C. left I spent most of my time in bed and my back was hurting so much that one day I took the mattress out from the bed frame and just put it on the floor. After that my back hurt less but because the mattress was on the floor getting up became unbearable for a reason that I only half understand, and the bed frame was preventing me from walking around the mattress, well I could walk around it but I had to be very careful because I kept bumping into the feet of the frame and hurting myself. One day, M. came round, we'd finally made peace. And we'd got our closeness back. It was like we'd never been apart.

She put the bed frame on the other side of the room so that I'd stop bumping into it and I wondered how I'd never thought of that myself but I realised that of course it's the sort of thing I don't think about because I'm not a practical person, except for sometimes.

It even happened that one day I was staying with a friend in a room in a dodgy seaside hotel in France and neither of us could get to sleep because the toilet flush wouldn't stop running, and so I went to look inside the cistern. I put a bit of towel inside it somewhere and, thank God, we were able to sleep afterwards, and my friend couldn't believe it and she always brought it up afterwards, about how practical I'd been for once in my life. And so whenever we felt like having a laugh we reminded each other of the story and we laughed and said, yes how practically minded. Now we don't laugh together because we're angry at each other and that's just how it is. We could have been angry with each other for a long time before that, especially me at her, or at least that's what I think, she must think the opposite but it's not up to me to put myself in her place anymore and to think about what she might be thinking because now we're angry at each other and I think we always will be, in any case that's how it is right now and although lots of things make me feel sick bizarrely this doesn't, and I think that's because I really must have been angry and because we don't see each other anymore because we're angry I'm not angry anymore, but only because we don't see each other anymore and so she can't give me new reasons to be angry. I loved her so much but now I don't. I loved her so much, she must have loved me too but as soon as someone else was in the picture, as soon as she had a new man I mean, the love that she had for me no longer counted for so much and I suffered in silence, but I could understand her so well that I didn't want to show her I was suffering so whenever I saw her I smiled so much that my cheeks hurt. I pretended that everything was all right and so did she. But nothing was all right anymore, at least for me, so I went off somewhere and absorbed myself in other things, like making a film, and I stopped feeling hurt about everything. I was so absorbed that I became happy and that really is a brilliant feeling that doesn't happen very often but when it does I feel like I'm flying, that I no longer have my feet on the ground and suddenly it's even easy for me to go to the supermarket.

But the worst thing about this friend I was angry with was that as soon as the man was out of the picture for one reason or another she came back to see me and then it all started over again and with a new man and everything else and that smile that hurt my cheeks, yes, the whole thing again and of course I could understand her, I could understand the whole thing very well and I knew that's how things would be and so it all started again and I went off to do something and life became liveable again. And when life is liveable you don't think of every day as being one day closer to death, not at all. You just think that life is liveable and that life is beautiful and you make the most of it and don't sleep as much. You make the most of it and you live. Everything contributes to this living and you can laugh over nothing.

Now we're not angry with each other anymore. Luckily. I've known her for so long, we were young and wreaked havoc together and lots of other things too, we can't stay angry at each other for ever, but things haven't been the same since. It really is a shame, an email exchanged every so often is all that's left. But it's a start and maybe one day we'll see each other again and it'll be just like before.

I should have known from her emails. Already at the start, before anything had happened between us, there was already a discernible jealousy disguised as humour. I could only see the humour. I was wrong.

I've always hidden it when jealousy overwhelms me. Always. And I've had my reasons, plenty of reasons to be jealous and to suffer but whenever my time has come I've said nothing. For example, more often than not I've been left for a boy, before being taken back and then rejected again, and I've let it all happen with a smile. It was stupid and even now when I think about it I say to myself, I shouldn't have. Shouldn't have gone about it like that. But it had become second nature to me.

One day I even wanted to kill myself but while smiling, the most important part was not forgetting to smile, as if what I was about to do was a meaningless act. Luckily it was because I survived. I've survived everything up until now and I've often wanted to kill myself. But I told myself, I couldn't do that to my mother. Afterwards, when she's not around.

Today someone is ringing at the door. It's not even nine and I'm still dozing because of the jetlag, after all I've just got back and I've had a terrible time trying to get to sleep.

It's Sunday. I think maybe it's C. but no, it can't be her. This time isn't like all the others when she'd turn up without warning, without me wanting her to.

I'm only half dressed. I've already had my morning coffee, I'm running a bath. I won't answer it. They ring again. I ask who it is again, I can't bear to open the door, I ask who is it again. A woman's voice replies, it's the exterminator. I say, everything's OK now. I'll probably be overrun by cockroaches now. Oh well.

Oh well, she's no longer there, it's only me who'll suffer and tomorrow is still far off.

She left the apartment. After all that. All that meaning thousands of loving emails exchanged, future plans, laughter and tears, more and more tears.

I'd told myself, I don't love her anymore, it's better that way, and I was starting to become scared of her. I'd said to her, I don't love you anymore, she'd said, that's not possible. I'd looked at her. Then I'd turned away. If someone had said that to me I would have believed them. Not her.

The door rings again. I open it. Another present has arrived. This really is one too many. So I put off opening it. I still don't know what it was.

When I'd asked my sister what sort of wedding present I should give my niece she told me, just bring some money. So I'd brought some, I thought it was a lot but when I gave it to my sister I understood that it wasn't very much at all. I've never known how to give presents. So I'd ended up feeling sad and a bit uncomfortable.

I've never known how to give presents and whenever C. gave me things I could barely look at them or if I did I was pretending, to make her happy. But really I never saw them.

I remember that my father would always give an envelope with money in it as a wedding present and it was less money than I'd given. But that was such a long time ago that maybe it was worth more, who knows.

When I got back after she had gone, I got into the habit of wandering around the neighbourhood.

The man who sells cigarettes asked me, where's your daughter?

The landlady, what happened to C.?

The concierge, where's C. and the dog?

The Hispanic neighbours, and C.?

When I wasn't wandering around the neighbourhood I stayed in bed. I took sleeping pills.

I didn't buy anything to eat, I finished what was left in the apartment, pasta, rice, at the beginning I ate them with tomato sauce, then without.

My nose was still hurting or at least I felt like it was.

And I said to myself, this is better, I didn't love her anymore, we were hurting one another. But was it true I didn't love her anymore. Did I still love her. Do I still love her. I couldn't tell. I was thinking about her a lot in any case. Especially when I accidentally came across something she had bought or when I drank coffee from one of her bowls.

Yes, and now, months later, I'm still surrounded by a few things that she forgot to put in her boxes. A light blue T-shirt. A pink one too and her trainers. A pair of her trousers that I wore then quickly washed. I didn't want to ruin her trousers on top of everything else. She must be missing them.

I remember one day in New York I phoned my mother who had just returned to her house in Brussels after all those months in Mexico, and she told me, bursting with energy, I feel alive! I feel so alive! She was almost shouting.

I was also feeling better, I thought I had fully prepared myself for her death, fully prepared myself to feel nothing, but when she said that, the heaviness that had been weighing on my shoulders, and on my stomach, that heaviness suddenly lifted.

I thought, really I was just kidding myself.

Really I wasn't ready at all.

When I got back to Paris there was still a pile of things that C. had left behind. I thought, I should send them back to her. I sent her an email saying I was in Paris, that I was going to sort out her things and send them back. There was still quite a lot.

I wondered if there was anything she didn't need. It doesn't really matter, I'll pack it all up anyway.

She wrote back, yes, I want it all back. The reason I left some of my things there was so that I could take it to New York in stages to avoid spending too much in one go. I also left some of my music books in your bedroom. They're there on the window sill on the far right if I remember correctly. I thought to myself, just as well, I'll have more air in the apartment. I don't want anything left in my life that reminds me of her, not in Paris or in Harlem. Without all the leftover debris I'll never think about her again and I'll be very happy.

I still don't know whether the light blue bathrobe is hers. Maybe.

It can't be mine. So maybe it's hers. But I feel good wearing it after my bath. It suits me. I like it. But if it's hers I'll give it back. I'll give everything back. I'll fold it all up. I'll fold it neatly. She'll feel as though all of her things have been put away and folded with care and maybe even a certain kind of love. Not the same kind of love as before, luckily.

When I've sent her all her things I won't have any more reason to email her. That'll be it. And emailing was the part I liked most.

It had started strangely and very quickly it became true love but it only existed in this strangeness, not in life I don't think and then she, and me too, we destroyed it. That's all we did.

I packed up the boxes and brought them down from the

first floor to the garage so that it would be easier. A friend was going to take everything to her. She would use it as an excuse to make a short trip to London. She likes London. I don't. Especially not those streets where everything looks the same. Especially not those dark basement flats which look out onto ugly back gardens where dogs go and piss in the morning, in any case that's what C.'s dog did, and probably not just that. But I don't want to know about it. Now she's in an attic in Zone 3 so she probably has to take her out.

My friend who loves London will travel with C.'s nomadic boxes. All that remains of C.'s possessions. She doesn't have much. Books, the ones she'd used to write her thesis, DVDs, T-shirts, a swimsuit, the one she wore the summer we went to Greece, and several pairs of trainers. I can't stop myself from thinking about her ankles in these trainers one last time. I manage to stop myself from thinking about the rest. Except for one book, the one that's called *The Gift*, which gives me the chills. I say to myself, I'm not capable of giving this back. And then I remember the rest. And that by giving everything back I'll get myself back.

When my friend got to London she didn't see C. It was C.'s friend who let her in. She got the feeling C. was hiding somewhere upstairs in her attic.

One day I received an email. She was asking for my help. She'd lost her passport, all her money, she had nothing left, everything had been stolen.

I sent her some money.

Then I received another email saying that she'd been hacked.

When she found out I had sent some money she wrote something ending with kiss you. *Je t'embrasse.*

I hesitated for a long time, I said to myself, I'm not going to reply with kiss you, or things might start up again. I said take care. *Prends soin de toi*, or something like that.

She wasn't happy. I don't remember in what circumstances she wrote, you'll always be special to me. I replied, don't, you'll make me cry. I've cried a lot too, you know, she replied.

No. I'm not going to reply. I won't reply. I'll stop replying.

Yes, I'll see you Tuesday. This is what I said to my mother who can hear me very well for once.
Will you stay for a few days?
Yes, until Friday or Saturday morning.
I woke up too late.
I missed my train.
Finally, I'm alone again.

I realise that I need to be here in my apartment, alone. I haven't done this for a long time. I no longer want to leave.

I phone my mother to swap the four days this week for a whole week next. She says, you're tired. Yes, I am tired.

Tiredness always gets you off the hook.

And I've really only just got back. Home, I mean. I have so much to do. I have things to do too, you know. I have all these papers and letters and payments. I understand, I have the same, it's unbearable. But my cousin is helping you, isn't she?

Yes she is, luckily, but I still can't stand it. It frightens me. I'm frightened of this sort of thing. Everything that might be called administrative frightens me. I think, me too, but I say, what's the worst that could happen? The payments go out automatically from your bank.

But the hospital in Mexico cost a lot and I'm entitled to a repayment but I have to answer so many questions. So I say again, but my cousin is helping you, isn't she. Yes, she's helping me but I have to be there and help her answer all the questions, she doesn't know everything that happened to me there. No of course not, but the questions will be those standard ones where you just put the same thing over and over. Anyway, you just have to tell the truth, it's better that way. But I can't remember what happened.

I don't know what else to say, I can't remember what happened so well anymore either.

Then she says, it's like a black hole. I understand. I tell her, I really do understand. I can't count the number of times I've had to get on a plane to say goodbye to her. I feel like I've spent my whole life on planes.

Luckily whenever I got to my sister's house there'd be the dog and the dog, pure white, would sleep on my bed with me and calm me down. They say that about dogs, that they take things on.

Her previous dog had been run over by a car, it was my niece's dog and she'd cried a lot. C. had this kind of love for her dog too.

C. had saved her at birth, and that was the only reason this dog existed.

C. loved animals and would have become a vet but her mother wanted better for her.

The idea of becoming a vet had reminded her of the country life she'd got away from and that's not what she wanted for her daughter.

When I was young I didn't like dogs but when I got one it was fantastic. I was madly in love with this dog and when he died I called up my mother sobbing hysterically.

I'd never cried like that before.

C. had lost her mother very young. When H. had asked what effect this had on her, to lose her mother like this to a serious illness, she'd just said, no comment.

It was that evening or maybe another, another one like that one, that she'd said to me, you won't leave me, will you. I'd said no, never.

I imagined her, all alone without a mother. How had she coped.

Sometimes she talked to me about it. Not often and I was scared to ask her questions but I knew that it was from a serious illness and that it was genetic. So I said to her, we'll go to the hospital together for the tests, but we never did.

She never learned to drive either.

She never wrote her book.

She was always scrutinising me from over her papers, that's why.

She was too busy.

She used to say, it's normal to be a bit jealous. A bit, maybe, but not for no reason.

I have my reasons.

This would go on for hours. Hours of heartbreak.

I could feel myself shutting down. I could never get used to those hours. I tried but I couldn't.

It's easy to cry over a dog. I've never screamed and cried as much as when my dog died. Even though he died of old age whereas my niece's dog had only just been born. Though when I say that my dog died of old age that's not strictly true, his kidneys had become blocked and L. and I would take him to the veterinary acupuncturist who'd stick these huge needles into him. The dog would look at us as if to say, do you think this will help and should I

just go along with it, but he could see from our eyes that it was a good thing and so he just lay back and went along with it.

One day the vet told us, there's nothing more we can do but I'm going to try one last injection, and for two days the dog stopped dragging himself around and making his horrible pained cries, I phoned L. who was away, the dog is better the dog is saved, thank God. Oh I was so relieved. And I told the dog, come, come say something to L., and I said to L., talk to him, the dog listened, L. didn't say anything but her silence reassured him.

The next day, and I think it began during the night, the dog started crying in pain again, I stroked him, I did everything and anything, I spoke softly into his ear, he seemed not to hear me very well anymore and he screeched. I phoned L. and said to her, this time it's really the end please come home, I don't want to go to the vet alone. She came back as quickly as she could. And that was it. Well, not exactly, the vet injected him with LSD first so he would die happy and we saw him relax little by little and give us a look of contentment, then he went to sleep for ever.

At that time I was still living with L. and I will always regret that time even though now I don't really anymore, not like I did before anyway. L. needed to experience new things and so did I, so I can understand. And then it became a different time.

M. was there, she was there with me and me with her. There were two of us. Well, she had children so we were more than two.

I really do understand why L. needed to experience new things but it's something so intimate that I can't bring myself to write about it. I won't forget L., who is still important to me and probably always will be.

Deep down, L. is family. Deep down, aside from my sister and my mother, I have a family. I know why L. needed someone else and sometimes I think, I could have given her what she needed. I still think that to this day but you can't go back and change things and I probably wouldn't have been able to give it to her anyway. Now L. lives a few minutes' walk from me, I mean when I'm in Paris and she is too, because she travels a lot for work.

And whenever we do happen to meet up in Paris, she brings me the Russian tea I like and also organic food because she knows that I never buy anything for myself and that I just eat in the local restaurant which is good but the food is unhealthy and full of germs and other bad things. And sometimes I go and eat at her apartment, she makes wild rice and tofu and vegetarian pâté and when we eat together it always tastes so good. No matter the food it always tastes good and we're happy together. After the meal I'm tired so I fall asleep in her bed in front of the flatscreen TV I once bought her as a present, even though I rarely give presents, and she works. She's a terribly hard worker, she's good at concentrating and has an incredible memory. I'm the opposite. Once I even made a film about laziness where I played myself as a lazy woman and she played herself as a hard worker and the film starts with the words, get up lazy one. I don't like being so lazy, I'm actually ashamed of it, but I have to own up to the fact that I'm becoming lazier and lazier by the day and have less and less of a desire to do anything. And that's where my laziness comes from.

Every step I take in my apartment in Paris makes me happy. Breathing there makes me happy. Going upstairs and downstairs makes me happy. As does throwing out old newspapers. Books I won't read again. Old invitations. Changing light bulbs. Buying new lamps. Sitting down here and there and getting up again. Listening to people shouting in the street. Then looking to see what's going on. Two tall guys are at each other's throats, shouting. Everyone on the street is watching, no one is doing anything about it. I think, they're going to kill each other. I decide to call the police. Two cars arrive very quickly, the police get out, separate the men, talk to them, then it's over. The two men even end up laughing.

Everything calms down.

Rifling through my drawers just now I've discovered three vest tops, one white, one black, one burgundy, will this ever end.

I smooth them out. Fold them.

If she were here to see this she wouldn't believe her eyes. She's never seen me do this. In general I throw everything into a suitcase. Maybe that's what she meant when she called me *self-involved*, not giving a shit about anything. About her suitcase along with everything else.

Clara is smoking outside on the balcony with me.
 In the evening she watches the TV with my mother.
 My mother needs company.
 She's had company since she came back from Mexico.
 Now she can't bear to live alone after so many years of living alone. All that is over, luckily Clara left Mexico to come and live with my mother.

Clara says she can't sleep at night for all the noise my mother makes.

In the morning she wakes up late to find my mother alone battling with a piece of toast, battling because of her broken left shoulder which will always be broken.
 She just about manages to make herself a cup of coffee using all her might.

My mother has got up from her electric wheelchair. She says that she feels refreshed and that she'll sit back down and wait for the carer to arrive.
 Will you let her in? Yes, of course.

She lies down in her armchair and groans. She groans at regular intervals. She never stops.

She'll have to go and buy me some bread. Yes. I'll tell her.

Haven't you got some pills to take?

Yes, I'll take them.

She groans. If only these groans would stop.

Yesterday she got so many compliments. She's doing much better and her hair has grown back. A miracle. And she has fewer wrinkles.

But she can't cut up her meat with her shoulder broken, or anything else for that matter. Yes, that's what doing much better looks like.

Because before it was even worse. And now it's a bit better. Or maybe I'm just dealing with it better.

Leave the kitchen door open will you, I need air.

We can't go out today but I need air. Luckily we went out yesterday. I ate a huge ice cream and took the air and looked at people. Respectable people.

Yesterday I didn't have my shower so today I'll ask the carer to help me take one. That'll be refreshing.

I can't do it on my own. I can't get dressed or undressed. Now even my right shoulder is starting to give me grief.

Have you seen the new carpet, it's at least four centimetres thick, that way if I fall I'll do myself less harm. It was your sister's idea to have it fitted. But now when you come in you have to make sure you take off your shoes straight away because I don't want to get my new carpet dirty. Yes, straight away.

And you mustn't smoke inside anymore, because it makes me choke, if you want to smoke you can go out onto the balcony.

Yes, I will.

I go and put a chair on the balcony and smoke a cigarette.

Finally, here she doesn't need an oxygen mask, or blood transfusions, or B12 injections.

Here she feels better. She's starting to forget a bit, that's all. And only sometimes.

But something has definitely changed, she no longer wrings her hands when she's anxious.

She doesn't wait by the window anymore.

Something in the atmosphere of the house has changed.

It's more bearable. I don't know why. It's the same but it's not. My mother is starting to live again. And when she puts on lipstick her lips no longer look like they're bleeding. I'd even say that it suits her. Probably because her cheeks are less green.

She says to me, you're pale. Yes, I know, the doctor in New York said that I'm anaemic.

Ah like me, I'm still anaemic.

He also said that I've got a vitamin D deficiency.

It's because of the sun. There isn't any. And she laughs.

I bought my mother some white flowers. It's so grey here in the apartment.

But with flowers maybe we'll feel it less.

We're making an effort. It isn't working very well.

I have nothing to say. My mother is complaining. Tell me something.

But what? Whatever you want, what you're up to right now. Tell me anything.

Ok, I'll try. But nothing, absolutely nothing, springs to mind, or to my lips.

It makes her sad. Me too. I'm having a bad day.

It'll pass.

Let's talk. But how to fill the silence. What do you want

me to tell you. Anything, it's all interesting to me.

She goes to lie down and I hide myself away in the little bedroom where the ironing is piled up.

I return to see her and say, why don't we make a list.
Let's write a list. The list is for shopping. Every day there's shopping to be done. Of course it's the carers who go and do it and they don't always make good choices. But sometimes they do.

Yes, but I don't have any ideas, says my mother.
So why don't we go to a restaurant for a change.
Yes, my mother says, we've not been to a restaurant in a long time.
In the restaurant she ate everything. Drank everything. A big steak with peppercorn sauce, fries, bread, butter. A big glass of red wine.
I cut up her meat as if it were the most natural thing in the world. But apart from saying that everything tasted good and that this restaurant is always good and that there are people who travel a long way to go to this restaurant, we had nothing to say.
She returned home full up. Not too far to walk. The restaurant is just on the corner.
I wanted to help her with the stairs but she chose the ramp, her body turned in on itself, twisted over, disarticulated, and she climbed the few stairs. Bravo, I said.
I went to bed.
In silence.
A heavy silence.
I got up, I saw my mother wasn't sleeping, I went to sit next to her and told her about New York, not in detail but it was recognisably New York.

She looked at me without judgment.

And she said, I'm happy that you're back together with M.

I hope you won't hurt her again.

No, never.

She's a good person, I've only met her once but I know she's good. Good and kind. I can sense these things.

You know, when I was very young I spent months exchanging letters with an Israeli soldier. That was my life at the time. A life lived through letters. I never went to meet him. I just missed the letters, that's all.

Then I met your father. In the flesh. And I stopped missing the letters. And you never wrote to him again? No. And you don't know what happened to him? No. And you never think about him? No. What if he's dead? Well I'll never know. So if he was dead you wouldn't feel a thing? You know, at the time I didn't know how to love. The letters were my way of learning, that's all. But how did you meet him in the first place, I mean you must have met him once? Yes, in passing, just at an evening event, he was a friend of someone I knew. All I can tell you is that he had very black hair, very black eyes and a big moustache. You still remember that? No but one day he sent me a photo and that's what I remember thinking. And because I still have the photo I remember, without it I wouldn't.

But you've never told me about him before.

No, what for? Deep down, it didn't matter. They were just letters, beautiful letters but letters all the same.

So letters don't count? That depends, but at that time in my life nothing could touch me. It was all the same to me.

But after that you became more sensitive. Yes, I was sensitive to your father's kindness. Are you saying that you didn't fall in love. No, after all that, after all that had happened to me, it was his kindness that counted most.

But when you were young you were always falling in love.

Yes, that was before. Before, everything seemed possible, even falling in love.

I'm going to go back to bed. Yes, go back to bed. But it's good to talk, don't you think?

Yes, it's good. But you rarely want to talk. Yes, I know, sometimes I shut down or have nothing to say.

But you don't have to have something to say in order to speak. You can just say something then something else, that's how people talk.

You know, I love to talk. Yes, I know that maman. I know, sometimes I end up repeating myself. Don't worry, it doesn't matter.

But sometimes I think that it does matter and that you can't stand it. Sometimes I can't stand it but sometimes I don't mind it.

When I can't stand it it's just because I'm in a bad mood and when I'm in a bad mood I can't stand anything.

So decide to be in a good mood then.

My sister loves L. because L. is like family to her, and she loves M. for other reasons, just because.

I tell her, I have some regrets about C.

And some pain too.

I skinned a lamb while it was still alive.

Now I'm bleeding.

Stop it. It's such a lovely day.

All right, I'll stop.

In Mexico, after she'd been taken into hospital again and after she'd got out of hospital again and when I'd seen her on Skype from New York, she looked like she didn't recognise me anymore so I shouted, maman, it's me maman, but she wasn't making eye contact and she seemed not to recognise me.

I said to myself, maybe deep down she's never recognised me. I thought, she's more real to me when she doesn't recognise me than when she's shouting that she loves me. I said to myself, that's my real mother there. Later on she told me that it was because of her blurred vision.

Another day in Mexico, when she'd stopped needing her oxygen mask, we took her out of the apartment. It was on one of the rare days when we took her out and it was because there was a screening of my latest film. She couldn't hear any of the film because her hearing aid had started to hurt but she'd seen the images and seen me get up on stage and answer a few questions and she'd seen that the reaction had been warm that day. When she'd finally managed to join me in the back of the car with the help of her grandson who'd carried her in, she said to me, my daughters, my daughters have everything. Me, I had nothing but the camps. It was the first time she'd said that. At other times she'd just said that she was happy and that everything had been wonderful, and suddenly there was this.

So I thought to myself again, this time she's speaking the truth, not the truth, but her truth, and it was horrible. But it was better for me, and for her, that it was said. And I didn't blame her for it. Not at all. It was better but I was still speechless, what could I say to that. I remember thinking, it's not fair, she had a life before the camps and a life after the camps, she even had fun sometimes and then she had us, her two girls, and I think she was also happy with my father who was a calming influence.

My father accepted it all and didn't seem to share her anxiety. He accepted the fact that she always wanted to be early for the train and he accepted the fact that she would start packing her bags a week before they left to go anywhere and he would never say anything about it. Yes, he accepted her anxiety and didn't say anything about it. He didn't even seem to notice it even though it was very noticeable but he acted like he didn't notice a thing and that it was all normal. But I would say, it only takes an hour to pack your bags and anyway you know exactly what you're taking and you never forget anything, unlike me.

I like to be prepared. She could well have said, I like to be prepared for anything and especially for the worst because the worst was something she had experienced, but she just said, I like to be prepared. Don't we know it. I would snap back unkindly and I thought that I was joking but that's not the sort of thing my mother would have found funny. The opposite, in fact. It shook her and made her anxiety worse so I'd say, do what you like. My father didn't say a word, he played the part of someone who didn't notice and that was probably the best thing he could have done.

I hate doing things in advance, I leave everything to the last minute when I have no choice but to do it, so of course I end up forgetting lots of things but it doesn't really matter.

I hate being prepared, I prefer to get up very early on the day I'm leaving and throw everything into a suitcase without looking. Without folding things up, without putting shoes in shoe bags. I throw all my medicine around because I take a lot of medicine. I have to because of my illness and my insomnia. And if I'm unlucky enough to forget one or other of my medicines I have to phone the pharmacy in Paris so they can send me some replacements and luckily my pharmacist is forgiving and knows that if I don't take my medicine my illness might flare up and then I would have to be locked away. My mother never forgets a thing but at what price, now I know the price she's paid for never forgetting anything. But it's a bit late for all that.

My sister doesn't forget anything either and she always travels with so much luggage. Her bags are filled to the brim and the more bags she has the fuller they are. I always say, I like to travel light, and my mother or my sister or even L. always says, just as long as you don't forget your medicine. Everyone says that and I'm sick of hearing it and I'm sick of my medicine and I'm sick of my illness and I'm sick of being locked up and I'm sick of insomnia, so I rarely forget my sleeping pills. People say, but which sleeping pills are they, they're very strong you know and people get used to them and end up having to take more and more just to get to sleep. And I tell them no, my new psychiatric pharmacologist told me you can't get used to these ones, they're not addictive and so there's no reason to be worried. But that's not entirely true.

Anyway I don't get worried unless I forget them because then I end up spending whole nights awake and sleep is very important for someone like me and even for other people too.

If I run out or I've forgotten to bring them with me I get into a panic, I go mad, I'd do anything for them, I've even shouted in an American pharmacy. I said that America wasn't a free country and that they'd even taken my fingerprints at the border like I was a criminal and that they had taken photos and I shouted that it was unconstitutional, an infringement on my privacy and lots of other things besides and the pharmacist, if you could even call her that, was shouting at me from behind her counter to calm down. But I couldn't calm down, I looked at everyone and I said, *America is not a free country*. I left the pharmacy and across the road I saw a pizzeria and I ate four slices of pizza in a row, they were so good I could have even ordered a fifth but I was starting to get a stomach ache and by some miracle I'd decided I'd had enough and anyway now I had become interested in the waitress who was talking to a young, fairly handsome man and I remember thinking they looked like two people in love, and that even if they weren't they obviously enjoyed spending time together and that if I were to order a fifth slice I'd disturb them. So I paid and left.

I was feeling fantastically good, well fed, and to top it all off I decided to go to the bar next door and drink a good glass of red wine.

I entered the bar which was lit only by the television in the corner and I saw just men. I pulled up a stool and ordered a glass of red wine. Unfortunately it wasn't very good but I drank it anyway, it would help wash down the four pizza slices. But it didn't help wash them down so I took a taxi home because going from east to west isn't so easy. You have to take a bus, get off the bus, and have change for the bus, so I took a taxi which took me back to the side of Harlem that I like best and lay down on my favourite bed, thinking, that poor pharmacist, I shouldn't have said those things to her, it's not her fault that she was the only person I could shout at. If I'd said all that at the border they would have sent me straight back to France just like France is doing with its immigrants and undocumented workers, not without giving them a good beating first sometimes.

My mother has always told me that a good little smack works better than anything else where children are concerned. But the smacks she gave me were so soft that I couldn't feel them. I was a little devil but my mother was an immigrant so she'd seen those before. I said to myself, one day I'll go back and see the kind pharmacist and apologise but even so I'll tell her that deep down I believe everything I said. I know you don't always have to say what you're thinking. Sometimes it's better to stay quiet and not to say anything, but I have difficulty with that. As soon as I think something when I'm with other people I tell them what I think and they're always better educated than me so they only humour me. But deep down I know what they're thinking, especially when it comes to well educated French people and sometimes Belgians too.

But I think the most educated people are also the most hypocritical. That's something I've known for a long time, since the first year I attended a secondary school for the children of the well educated. The school was still girls-only at that time and these well educated girls had already learned how to be hypocrites and always say exactly what they were supposed to. That's something they'd learned at home. And these girls had mothers who'd also gone to this secondary school for the well educated. They always got good grades in manners but I didn't because I thought it was better not to be a hypocrite. Another word I learned at school. I never use this word anymore.

So one day I stopped saying what I thought and instead sat at my desk reading a book, that way I couldn't pay attention and wouldn't have anything more to say. I soon got caught, of course. The literature teacher sneaked up behind my desk and said, I knew it.

I was reading Radiguet and it was absolutely fascinating. I said to her, I'm reading a novel, it's absolutely fascinating. I don't doubt it, she said. Get out of my classroom. I couldn't have wished for a better response, I went out into the corridor with my book and continued to read. When I'd finished my book I didn't know what to do next so I went to the toilet. Usually you had to raise your hand, wait around for a teacher to spot you and ask yes, what do you want, and then you could ask if you could go to the toilet. Usually the response was either yes, no or not again. No, they never said not again in case you replied, I have diarrhoea. It would have been seen as crude to say that so teachers were scared to say not again. Though instead of saying not again, the teachers, who I now realise were all women, could have said, are you feeling ill, and in that case I would have replied, I'm feeling very well, actually, I just need to go to the toilet, it's a pretty natural impulse after all. But anything natural was frowned on in my school. The natural led you to a bad grade in manners. So sometimes I managed to rid myself of natural impulses, but often I forgot. Anyway, in this corridor I was finally able to go to the toilet whenever I wanted and that was a good start.

Later on the teacher who'd sent me out of class was the only one to speak to my mother with a bit of humanity, though that's not how my mother and I had understood it at the time.

She said to my mother, your daughter should be helping you out around the house or she'll pay the price for it later in life. My mother replied, but she dries the dishes and even puts them away sometimes. The teacher had replied, she should be doing more than that. It's for her head.

My mother had looked at her, thinking about what she'd

just said. And the teacher repeated, she should be doing more. My mother hadn't asked how I'd pay the price or what was wrong with my head. Still to this day I wonder how this teacher could have got it so right. Whenever my mother used the word head she was thinking about a full head of hair, that's all. She never spoke about the head as anything else.

I often think of this teacher when I wake up in the morning with a lump in my throat. On those days I start moving, tidying things away, going through the motions and even taking the rubbish downstairs before I've had my morning coffee, and I feel better.

None of the other teachers at school were like that. My mother wasn't prepared for it. At primary school all the teachers liked me and everyone knew it.

Some of the other children had even complained. They said, they like you. They like you more than the rest of us. You're the favourite. But it wasn't a middle-class school and the children hadn't heard of the Iliad or the Odyssey, and none of them had seen the Parthenon.

In my first month at secondary school my mother had been called in. Your daughter is unbearable, they'd told her. My mother, who could be called everything except a hypocrite, had replied, oh really, but she's lovely at home.

The class monitor hadn't known what to say. The mothers usually agreed with whatever was said, and they were never usually called in during their daughter's first month at school. My mother was the only one so she'd been seen straight away, which was lucky because she still had to do the shopping for supper and then the cooking. I was usually the one to lay the table and look after my sister but that wasn't difficult because my sister always came home from school in the same state she'd gone in. She never fell down or got her clothes stained. She never wanted to do her homework but that was understandable. She never hung out in the street after school, then again she was only four at the time. She was lucky. She went to a nursery where everyone was kind to her and I don't know why I said that she never wanted to do her homework because there was no homework at nursery. It was only later that she had homework she didn't want to do. And then I'd tell her, do your work, you have to, or you'll come to a bad end and end up having to sell shoes. Why shoes, she'd ask me, because I always said shoes and nothing else. Selling shoes like P. when she came back to Belgium.

But my sister was always even-tempered and that was all that mattered.

Especially when you're still very little.

As for me, I always hung around in the street after school because of love. Love makes you hang around. I used to walk a girl a couple of years above me to the Gare du Luxembourg. We would talk for a long time, she would miss one train, sometimes two, to talk to me for longer, even when it was raining. I can't remember what we talked about. Whenever it rained her long blonde hair became darker but it didn't matter. She always ended up getting on a train and I would always return home. I didn't know what love was at the time. But that was surely it.

Nothing ever happened between us but it was love and it was what made school bearable.

I would wake up at the crack of dawn every day to get to school early to meet her. We would rush to meet in-between our classrooms to talk just for five minutes. We had so much to say to each other. So it was worth it, even for five minutes. But it was never enough.

When she left school to get married it ended. A huge emptiness opened up inside. I did everything I could to skip school but the less I went the worse it became. Bleaker too.

She'd left school and also Europe for her husband. She'd gone to a hot, war-torn country. It's a country I like. It's the country of my ancestors, or so they say. She wrote to me a bit at first, but after that she must have forgotten. Later on I found out that she and her husband had separated. I don't know why. They were both so beautiful.

Sometimes I still wonder whether I should try and find her, because in the meantime I'd heard she'd returned to Belgium and was selling shoes in a small provincial town. And I'd often wondered what her life was like.

But I'd never come to any conclusions.

What sort of shoes and what did the little town look like and where might it be.

Later on I learned that it was Mons.

Mons was on the way to Paris and at the time the train still stopped there so I thought maybe one day on the way to Paris she'll get on the same train.

And I'll ask her for some shoes.

Anyway, I'd always liked the shoes she wore. They were nearly all the same style but in slightly different shades.

I remember her shoes and also her nightdress in transparent nylon.

One day she'd stayed overnight at my house and she'd slept in my bed in this nightdress.

We'd talked a bit in bed but not too loudly so as not to wake up my sister who was asleep in a different bed in the same room.

She fell asleep first. Later on I went out with a girl who looked just like her, or at least I thought she did except that she had light red hair. With her I knew it was love.

But not with P. I spent every break time with her in the big park belonging to the school and we would talk there too as we walked up and down the paths.

The park had big trees with no leaves, I don't know why but it always seemed to be autumn or winter.

The school was in the middle of this park which made it look like a château. I used to wonder whether châteaux had dungeons, but I don't think so.

I also remember that she had a little brother she never spoke about and whom I only saw once, at the wedding, and I don't remember what he looked like, except that he was a little brother and he had a crew cut.

Anyway at the wedding I didn't see a thing and I came back to Brussels from Paris with her parents, the husband was from Paris so the wedding was in Paris. I came back with them in their car, the parents and the little brother, and we arrived there at dawn. I remember feeling that it had taken all night. In the car her parents seemed happy with the wedding but were worrying over her little brother who still wet the bed sometimes but deep down it didn't really matter because they knew it was just a phase. And that was how I missed my Latin exam retake.

My cousin was a bit like P.'s little brother and everyone despaired of him even though they knew it was just a phase. Nobody knew what to do, least of all his mother because his mother was strange. People said strange in order to avoid the word mad. She would visit us every Wednesday with my cousin and my mother would close the door to the kitchen because she knew that my aunt was going to say strange things that she didn't want me to hear.

On Wednesday evenings my mother was exhausted and would say to my father, it's happening again. Whenever she said that I knew that my aunt was going to disappear into a clinic for a few months. And she would say, that's probably why he still wets the bed at his age, meaning my cousin. Everyone had forgotten that his father was good for nothing. It was all the mother's fault. Everyone had forgotten that if his father had been good for something my aunt probably would have had fewer strange things to say. But those things are always forgotten, and sometimes it's better that way. My father would often say, yes but she should never have married that good for nothing, he never said more than that but we guessed the rest and it wasn't worth talking about. And anyway I don't think my aunt was mad. No more than I am in any case. My cousin loved his mother. He still talks about her whenever we see him but we hardly ever do. He has his mother's eyes, but not entirely. Everyone says, he's done very well for himself all things considered, and in his line of work he's even made a bit of a name for himself. He works with pearls, he carefully sews pearls onto wedding dresses for the grande bourgeoisie and sometimes even nobility. And he draws. He's the first person in our family to do that.

My mother doesn't like hearing about pearls, which is probably why we don't see him very often. And probably also because she can see my aunt in his eyes and it makes her shudder.

My cousin lost his mother at a very early age. He'd only just turned ten and no one ever asked him what it was like to lose a mother so young, a mother who didn't want to live.

Sometimes at funerals, and I went to one not so long ago,

someone asks whether the parents of the dead person are still alive and everyone hopes that they're not because there's nothing worse than outliving your child.

At the funeral I went to not so long ago someone said to me, that's one of our generation on their way out. By that he meant that it might be our turn soon, but that's not what he said.

Someone else said to me, you must carry on. You will carry on, won't you.
She'd meant carry on making films. I replied almost automatically, yes, of course. And then I'd turned away. Why should I have to carry on. Why had I said yes, of course, so quickly. Because.
Afterwards I saw this person again and she'd grabbed my arm very tightly all of a sudden and I'd thought, now she's found another way of telling me to carry on. I hadn't moved, I'd waited for her to let go and finally she had and when I looked to my side a bit later on she was no longer there. I could breathe again.
Someone else said to me, it was a beautiful service all things considered. The all things considered said it all.
Though I found myself thinking, all things considered, that it wasn't worth the trouble of saying such things and then I thought, but it's because there's nothing that can be said.
So I looked at the three daughters of the man who had died and I thought, they're beautiful.
I never knew he had three daughters and, deep down, what had I really known about him. It was cold, I left, I went back home, it wasn't a long way. But it was cold at home too so I put myself to bed. I got a pile of blankets and duvets and got into bed but I was still cold.

I tried to remember something about the dead man, about the first time I'd met him. It was a very long time ago and he was so young and beautiful. Like his daughters. I don't know why but his daughters' beauty made me feel even sadder.

They were the sort of beautiful that made you want to cry but I hadn't cried, I hadn't been able to. Then I remembered the man who had talked about generations and I thought, this is the first time I've belonged, I belong to a generation. And that made me feel something.

A generation that had believed in everything, and especially in everything being possible. And among this generation, at the cemetery, there had been someone who I'd loved a lot, I'd even told him once, you're my brother.

He'd said, you're right. I still remember that.

Yes, I could still remember that.

He also had three daughters and one of them was crying. She was so young. Barely more than sixteen.

It was also at a funeral that my father had said to my mother, we should have had another child. I was standing near him and I heard him.

But it was too late, so he'd squeezed my mother's arm and walked with her through the tombstones. It hadn't been cold that day.

All that I've written I've now told M.

I'm sitting on the balcony of the house overlooking the sea and I'm happy with M.

I've known M. for a long time and it's taken me a long time to realise how much I love her.

We loved each other, we went our separate ways, I don't remember why, and now we love each other.

Even our shadows are in love when we walk.

CHANTAL AKERMAN

AFTERWORD

CHANTAL and her mother are making a list because every day the shopping needs to be done, even if neither of them feel like it today, even if Chantal never really feels like it. It is something that they know how to do together. One will suggest it to the other in order to generate a conversation: 'Let's make the shopping list.' And if Natalia forgets something, Chantal remembers: 'And I say automatically, pre-cut vegetables for the soup.' The list is a burden and an anchor. It's necessary and unbearable. It promises action, gestures towards the near future. A bag of floury potatoes, fromage blanc, butter.

These passages of itemising and repeating in *My Mother Laughs* pulse with the same cumulative dynamic of Akerman's films. They also remind you why film, with its ability to capture movement in time, was the medium that Akerman chose primarily to work in throughout her life. She wrote in parallel with and into and through her films, producing screenplays, essays and a small number of autobiographical texts of which *My Mother Laughs*, first published in France in 2013, is the last. She conceived some of her earliest films as novels, and later would adapt Proust (*La Captive* in 2000) and Conrad (*Almayer's Folly*, 2011) for the screen. But I don't think she wrote to be read, not exactly, not like this. Her writing has more often been spoken aloud, most of all in the voiceovers and dialogue of the films, but also the recorded text in her installation *Bordering on Fiction: Chantal Akerman's 'D'Est'*, and the autobiographical monologue *A Family in Brussels*, which was written to be performed by its author and published as a book and a recording.

Reading this book, I realise that I've come to know Akerman's texts mostly through the hybrid listening-reading-watching that you do when watching a subtitled film in a foreign language. Audio and visual perception overlap and tangle into something so complex and dense that its constituent elements are barely noticeable unless one is missing or out of place. So I'm reading and I realise I'm missing her recordings of voices. I'm missing her voices and missing her voice. I read and try to hear it: grainy, rounded, blunt. Softly percussive and descending in pitch at the end of each sentence as she reads the letters from Natalia in *News From Home* (1976). Raised and sharp so that Natalia can hear her over a Skype connection in *No Home Movie* (2015). Or in *From The Other Side* (2002), recounting in a low, anecdotal tone an apocryphal story about a woman who crosses the border from Mexico to the United States and one day simply disappears from her room, constructing a ghost story out of the brutal reality of displacement.

In *My Mother Laughs* Akerman addresses her need to write and the frustrations of writing. She annexes a space to write in a small bedroom in her mother's flat. Writing, she asserts, is 'the only thing that can save me' (though she says the same thing about smoking a cigarette on the balcony). She remembers the breathless pace of emailing and messaging her lover when they only knew each other online. But something's not working here. Things that should pass by or be absorbed stack up. Her epistolary relationship doesn't survive its transition to a flat in New York. Being able to write is a marker of functionality yet it somehow offers no release: 'I read through everything

I wrote and I felt very disappointed. But what can I do. I wrote it. It's there.'

'After a few days I re-read everything I had written.' This is Akerman as 'Julie', the protagonist of her film *Je Tu Il Elle* (1974), speaking in voiceover, after she has written her three-page letter to her girlfriend out onto six pages, rewritten it and edited it down to a few lines, while eating spoonfuls of sugar from a paper bag. Is she disappointed? She doesn't seem to be. She spreads the paper out on the floor in methodical piles, takes off her clothes, sleeps, waits. Days pass. Writing seems like a mad thing to do, a thing that keeps you in your room for a month with nothing to eat but a bag of sugar, wrapped in a jumper on a mattress while people walk past outside and what is there to show for it, just piles of paper, and in the end you go and see the girl you were writing to anyway. It also seems like a blissful thing to do, this thing that keeps you in your room until you're just edits and appetites. Akerman was 24 when she directed and acted in *Je Tu Il Elle* and time is elastic. There is time for you to be in the room with her and hitchhiking with her, and in bed with her and Claire.

There is time to be bored. Shortly before *Je Tu Il Elle* Akerman made *Le 15/8*, a short film in which a young woman – a Finnish houseguest of one of her friends – drifts around a flat in Paris while a voiceover talks about . . . I can't remember. Everything? Not much? Just how she feels that day in droning, heavily accented English. I saw the film just once and haven't seen it since, but afterwards I enthused about how boring it was, it was so massively boring, I loved it, I said. I was describing it to a friend who hadn't seen it. She doesn't do anything, I said. She sits around. She has a sandwich and licks the knife. That had been my favourite part, although I can't now remember whether she actually puts the knife in her mouth or runs her finger along the knife and licks jam or Nutella or whatever off her finger. Either way it is an icky, childish thing that you might do on your own in someone else's flat, bored and sleepy, eating because why not. The boredom of *Le 15/8* is not austere or bleak but sticky and erotic and funny, too – a to-do list with nothing on it, no pressure to be a good guest or tidy daughter, no need to be anything except a girl feeling bored, maybe sad, maybe not, eating jam off a knife. It was so, so boring, I kept saying, it was good because it was boring. But that didn't really describe the heavy late-summer tempo of the film. You kind of had to be there.

Film's command of time never seems more enviable than when you're trying to write about it. This is true of all moving image, perhaps, but especially of Akerman's early films, in which the viewer shares, rather than merely observes, the characters' experiences of time, whether that's Julie's self-imposed isolation in *Je Tu Il Elle*, the liminal zones of hotel rooms and train journeys inhabited by Anna in *Les Rendez-Vous d'Anna* (1978), or the metre of domestic time in Akerman's best known film, *Jeanne Dielman, 23 Quai du Commerce, 1080 Bruxelles* (1975), which charts three days in the life of a housewife and occasional sex worker, played by Delphine Seyrig. Some of these stretches of time are or seem to be unnaturally long, but unlike many minimal and durational artworks, their purpose is not to take the viewer outside their bodies and into a meditative trance, although this is not to say that they do not encourage a different type of heightened awareness. Instead the static or slowly moving shots draw the attention to what happens in these time zones, what happens to the bodies in those time zones, in which nothing much is supposed to happen. Who inhabits them? Girls, queers, shift workers, migrants, carers, old people, mothers: their voices and actions slowly emerge and harmonise with one another. Listen. Sometimes they actually sing. *La Captive*: Sylvie Testud and Sophie Assante are piecing together a duet from Mozart's *Cosi Fan Tutte* from their balconies in different apartment buildings. Testud as Ariane, the captive, is tentative, then confident, drawn briefly out of her isolation by the voice of the other woman, whom she can't see.

D'Est, Akerman's 1993 documentary about the changing post-communist landscapes of Poland and Russia, features long tracking shots showing the endless queues that people wait in at stations, outside post offices or on the street. This visual cliché of the 1980s Soviet city – the obedient subjects of totalitarianism waiting patiently in line – is revealed to contain complex dynamics, fragments of drama. People argue, sleep, read books, exchange food, group and regroup in clusters; children play, a young soldier smiles at the camera and an old man hides from it. In his book 24/7, Jonathan Crary notes how in *D'Est* Akerman portrays waiting as 'something essential to the experience of being together, to the tentative possibility of community. It is a time in which encounters can occur.'

For Crary, Akerman captured a vanishing period of shared temporal community before a new '24/7' era of privatisation and atomisation took hold in these countries. But he doesn't mention that Akerman is also visiting her mother's homeland. There is another vanished world in the film. Natalia was born in Poland and escaped to Belgium at the start of the World War Two. She was deported back to Poland and sent to Auschwitz, where both her parents died. After the war she returned to Brussels, where Chantal was born in 1950. A group of people gathered on a cold street or waiting in a line in a crowded municipal building might be a community, but it might equally be a community that is about to be forced apart and destroyed. Akerman presents you with the queues, obsesses over the queues, and you watch them, fascinated, lulled, tense, fearful. There is enough space in the time that the tracking shots take for multiple narratives and histories, for individual and collective memories, to be suggested.

In *Autor de 'Jeanne Dielman'*, a documentary shot by Sami Frey during *Jeanne Dielman*'s filming, Akerman and Delphine Seyrig have long discussions about the pace at which the director wants the actor to carry out various movements at the small kitchen table at which so much of the film takes place. 'It's not so much the duration, it's the sensation of time,' Seyrig proposes, running through her actions like a dancer in rehearsal, usually with a cigarette in her hand. She addresses domesticity like an anthropologist. It's clear she has never spent much time in the kind of kitchen where the cutlery is kept in a drawer that pulls out from the table that doubles up as a work surface. She and Akerman discuss how Jeanne would make a veal escalope, and it turns out that they themselves don't really know how to do it. Do you put the meat back in the fridge once it's coated? 'A good cook wouldn't do that.' 'Jeanne isn't a good cook.' Well, Akerman concludes, 'my mother says it's right – but I haven't asked my aunt.' The sensation of time expands to include a family and its female elders, those that are still here: mother-time, aunt-time, survivor-time, observed by Akerman in her mother's kitchen and transmitted through Seyrig's careful gestures.

Many such moments of what queer theorist Elizabeth Freeman calls 'temporal drag' occur in *Jeanne Dielman*, in the way that the film commemorates and re-performs a domestic, working class femininity that was already old at the time the film was made – but that I, born in the late 1970s but raised in an extended family of grandparents and great aunts, still faintly remember and feel traces of on my skin when I watch the film. These are tactile memories of materials and textures – polyester fibres, smooth tiles, dry hands, J cloths, the curve of an overstuffed chair, wood veneer, rough towels: 'Affective histories,' Freeman writes, which are 'practices of knowing, physical as well as mental, erotic as well as loving "grasps" of detail that do not accede to existing theories and lexicons but come into unpredictable contact with them.'

'But we still talk about those aunts, we think about them sometimes, often even,' Akerman writes in *My Mother Laughs*. 'At least, my mother and I talk about them and we laugh.'

For every film we understand as Akerman's, there are numerous co-creators: actors such as Seyrig or Aurore Clément in *Anna*, cinematographer Babette Mangolte, editor Claire Atherton and sound recordists and editors including Suzanne Sandberg, Dominique Dalmasso, Jean-Paul Loublier and many others. The films' complex rhythms and bright tonalities of sound and image emerge from these networks. Trying to capture such collaboratively made artworks in the solitary space of writing, you first try writing along with the film in an effort to understand the pace of the edits, the layering of the sound, but you start to feel like one of the self-involved men who talk to Anna in *Les Rendez-Vous d'Anna*, while she zones out, occasionally responding 'On le dit' ('So they say'), as they tell you all the different places they've lived or what they think about women. Your page fills with lists and more lists: sequences of actions (wash, peel, fold, knit, sleep), inventories of repeated objects, spaces and sounds (phone, train, brakes, corridor, shoes) and basic technical observations (slow pan, traffic high in mix). You make itineraries (Cologne, Brussels-Midi, Paris). Your notes read like Natalia's shopping list, or Jeanne's (eggs, mince, breadcrumbs, potatoes, coffee). Isn't writing supposed to be more than this?

Janet Bergstrom acknowledges a similar problem in an essay about *Jeanne Dielman*, published in the feminist film journal *Camera Obscura* in 1977. She notes that 'the temptation is to retell the plot step by step, as if the clarity of the succession of gestures and elisions carried with it an understanding of the film's strength and its importance to feminist filmmaking.' It's true, although I am tempted not so much to recount the plot as to endlessly note gestures and sounds, abstracting the film into a kind of spatiotemporal score or fixating on one repeating motif. The last time I watched *Jeanne Dielman* I became obsessed with the lights – Jeanne is forever switching them on and off, every time she leaves a room and enters or exits the hallway. She is doing this because she is thrifty and having the lights on costs money. But she is also telling us where to direct our attention and where we can't go. Over the course of two hundred minutes the click of the light switch and the corresponding illumination or obscuring of space comes to feel as important as the edits made in post-production. Placing, or appearing to place, this control in the hands of Jeanne gives her an agency that female subjects of films are rarely allowed. It's a small gesture of power, but a significant one, that even as her routine breaks down she decides what we see of it and where.

In an interview from the 1980s Akerman describes developing dialogue into 'a litany, a blah-blah-blah, repeatedly writing in phrases such as "because" and "and then" so that the dialogue becomes a refrain'; she relates this directly to the Jewish liturgy she heard and learned as a child going to Hebrew school and to synagogue with her grandfather. The psalmodic texture of this kind of speech is both comforting and enervating. Like making the shopping list or the endless repetition of household chores, it is a protective, keeping-going action.

'To say nothing, do nothing, mark time, to bend, straighten up, to blame oneself, to stand, to go toward the window, to change one's mind in the process, to return to one's chair, to stand again . . .' the Lebanese-American poet Etel Adnan writes in 'To Be in a Time of War' (2005). Adnan is confronted by daily reminders of the war in Iraq and then memories of other times of war as she catches sight of newspaper headlines or TV footage, but it can be borne as long as she keeps moving and doing. There is a resonance between these two queer women writing from and through histories of violence, displacement and exile that I perceive as something heard and felt, an insistent rhythm that, deriving from different sources and traditions, nonetheless drives their work forward. There is some irony in Adnan's avoidance, as there is in Akerman's characters' and Akerman's own avoidance, as they circle around trauma, try to ignore the war. But there is also a profound recognition that this is how artists can, perhaps should, deal with a reality that cannot be represented. 'I passed the town where my mother comes from. Didn't see it, didn't look,' Akerman writes in the text that accompanies the installation version of D'Est.

It feels glib to say that Akerman wrote and directed from a time of war, that her characters' strategies of lassitude, refusal, motion, repetition, list-making, disassociation, escaping, travelling, itemising, singing are all ways of being in a time of war. That her own formal strategies, which enact rather than merely portray these actions, could be likewise. It feels obvious to say that it is always a time of war. We all know this. Akerman, repurposing surveillance footage of border patrols in *From the Other Side*, filming desert roads in Israel on her phone and blowing the footage up into the multi-screen digital onslaught of *Now*, her final installation work, never stops knowing it. Never stopped knowing it. Never stopped.

And yet in those last statements – *My Mother Laughs* and the film that is its companion piece, *No Home Movie* – Akerman acknowledges that something has to stop, or maybe she doesn't, maybe she fights it but it stops anyway. Bodies, a body – the mother's body – failing and rallying, viewed in a sudden new proximity. The daughter's body, uncomfortable in a home that's not her home. This is caretime, which can change pace and perspective suddenly, with long, quiet days then hastily booked trips and fractured nights. 'I'm not ready and maybe I never will be,' Akerman writes of this new mode of waiting. But in her final film she articulates it through a deeply affecting, affective use of those ubiquitous digital tools that we are supposed to see as so damaging to our relationship with time and each other.

The queues in *D'Est* are compelling not only because Akerman allows them time but also because she insists on space, a sort of formal, painterly distance between the camera and the subjects, a space between different registers of experience, between the seen and the felt, between the image and the sound and the body. But I started writing about Akerman because of how she bridged these spaces, or more accurately, how she seemed to try and bridge them and was not deflected, despite all the things in the way. It was because I went to the cinema one afternoon to see *No Home Movie*, filling a few hours between working and caring for my mother, who was ill at the time, who is elderly, who was born a few years before the start of World War Two. I started thinking about all the things in the way and their possibilities.

No Home Movie begins with a long static shot of a tree on a hillside blown and bent by a strong wind, filmed on a cheap digital camera, maybe a phone. I wrote a list.

> The first thing you hear in No Home Movie is the sound of wind blowing through a tree and across a valley. The first thing you hear in No Home Movie is wind distorting the sound of wind. The first thing you hear in No Home Movie is wind distorting the sound picked up by the microphone. The first thing you hear is the microphone, which is part of a camera. The first thing you hear is the camera.
>
> The first thing you hear in No Home Movie is the impact of wind on a hand-held camera. But is it on the camera, or in, or both: 'It may also be possible for wind to leak through holes cut for switches and generate noise inside the body too,' an instructional PDF downloaded from the Microphone Data website warns the recordist. The first thing you hear is the hand holding the camera. The first thing you hear is the body.

When this kind of digital excess bleeds through the cinema screen and its carefully calibrated sound system it can feel radical and disruptive. At the deep level of process as well as through the senses, noise and distortion resist a smooth, orderly understanding of time. In No Home Movie the extraneous artefacts of time-based recording technology are magnified, visually and sonically, and they call attention to other kinds of extraneity – other things that get in the way of communication or recording or representation, or that are supposed to be invisible or inaudible. Those artefacts – the distortion, glitch, interference, light bleed and so on – remind you that intimacy is both transmitted and frustrated by technology. Technology not only enables but creates intimacy.

The film theorist Mary Ann Doane has written about how the home movie was a technological development from the family photograph and how it was supposed to do the same thing, show what a family looked like – show a family what it looked like to itself – and perpetuate a visual ideal of family life to be reproduced and emulated. A 'no home' movie, a queer home movie, works against this inexorable reproduction through an excess of images, through the 'wrong' images, accidental images, a lack of continuity and order.

In an interview after Akerman's death by suicide in 2015, Claire Atherton, who edited *No Home Movie*, talks about how they had gone through the many hours of footage together: 'After making those images, she didn't know what they were. Some of them were on memory cards, phone, computers, it was messy. It was very complicated. In the scene where they eat, she just leaves the camera outside the kitchen and goes and talks with her mother. She forgot about it.'

No Home Movie includes a number of Skype conversations between Chantal and Natalia in which technical and operational glitches happen and long goodbyes leave uneven edges. The Skype call, with its drop-outs and time-lags and weird overdriven bursts of noise, equates neatly with the characterisation of digital media as atomising and alienating, the implication being that these communications, mediated through screens that flatten affect, are not only inferior but detrimental to 'real' relationships. But Akerman shows that connection can be made not despite but because of or even through glitch, and that the screen is a fine mesh that in fact clarifies, sharpens rather than obscures emotion. You notice how the conversations between them that take place at the kitchen table are just as vulnerable to a different kind of glitch and interference. Something too loud, or too absent, or an absence too loud to be voiced, gets in the way. In both cases, the glitches are not smoothed out but left in: Akerman stays with the interference. And Atherton says, of the editing sessions, with all their mess and multiple formats and found footage: 'We were building something, we were laughing. Sometimes it was sad, but it was happy.'

'I don't want everyone to hear the things I want to say to you,' Natalia says during one of the Skype conversations. As if the viewer will somehow catch not just the things that are said but the things that are not said but desired to be said. As if the things that are said aren't exactly the things she wants to say, but that they will be there somehow anyway, caught by the camera and the microphone, inscribed somehow by the apparatus that translates her words into data into signals. Her old beautiful face fills the screen of the laptop, a screen within a screen within a screen.

In *Tell Me* (1980), in which Akerman interviews a group of elderly Jewish women, Holocaust survivors like her mother, one of her subjects interrupts the story she is telling. 'I have so much to tell you, we could stay eight days and not finish all of it,' she says, the subtitles say. Eight days, three days, twenty-eight days, sixty-five years, eighty-six years, a generation, a century, twenty hours, two hours, a minute, a note, a breath, a footstep.

FRANCES MORGAN
London, July 2019

NOTE ON THE TRANSLATION

I LINGERED for a long time over videos of Chantal Akerman speaking English before translating the first sentence of *Ma mère rit*. I wanted to hear the grain and cadence of her voice in the hope of capturing it on the page. It's rare for a translator to have access to the writer in question speaking the target language, but as a filmmaker whose films were a fixture on the international festival circuit, Akerman was expected to give endless interviews in English. The YouTube interview I like the most is from the Venice Film Festival in 2011, where Akerman would have been presenting *Almayer's Folly*. Her voice is weathered from decades of smoking, hoarse and deep. She grew up speaking French and despite her experience speaking English, you can still see her wrestling with it, her lips contorting around each syllable like an early learner. She seems both playful and deeply aware of all that language can be and do. Akerman's Franco-Belgian accent often disguises the accuracy of her diction. While translating, I have occasionally had to stop myself from including the small Frenchisms that would, no doubt, have crept into her own translation of the text.

Akerman enjoyed speaking English because she felt completely uninhibited. As no one expected her to speak it well, she felt she was free to speak it badly. She sometimes found herself answering in English when asked about more philosophical subjects, and she wondered whether this unconscious impulse could be traced back to the shared roots of Yiddish and English: the language that would have been her first had it not been for the Holocaust. In *Ma mère rit*, Akerman constantly upends the rules of grammar, alternating between questions with and without question marks; deciding, seemingly arbitrarily, whether a new speaker should be introduced by name or not, though never with the use of speech marks. Tenses go against convention and are sometimes inconsistent – a relationship that has ended, for example, is mostly described in the past but sometimes creeps into the present. For the most part, I have kept the description of feelings in the present tense, and put the evocation of events in the past. But even this has felt like a slight betrayal of Akerman's rebelliousness.

The simplicity of Akerman's sentences is paradoxically the hardest thing to translate. It's a style described by Ivone Marguiles in reference to her film scripts as a 'hyperbolic literalness'. The sentences of *Ma mère rit* have childlike constructions and are often repetitive, with whole paragraphs duplicated across the text. I have been faithful to this simplicity, even when it seems less natural in English. This simplicity holds even when the content of the sentence contains deep hesitation and ambivalence. Akerman will begin with an almost naive 'je ne sais pas . . .' (I don't know); 'j'aime/je n'aime pas . . .' (I like/I don't like); 'je me dis que . . .' (I tell myself that) in order to say something emotionally significant:

> Je n'aimerais pas au fond qu'on me change de sang.
> Je ne sais pas pourquoi je tiens à mon sang. C'est un sentiment obscur et je n'aimerais pas le mettre en lumière.

> Deep down I wouldn't really like to have someone else's blood. I don't know why I care so much about my blood. It comes from a dark place that I don't want to uncover.

NOTE ON THE TRANSLATION

Often in Akerman a superficial reaction can precipitate a tortuous, half-disguised meditation on her depression. In *Ma mère rit* and elsewhere, Akerman refers to herself as an 'old child': mature before her time but unable, as an adult, to make a life for herself. Are these constructions the stylistic distillation of 'old childishness', where feelings can only be expressed after a remark that seems slightly flippant and throwaway? Or an extension of the her-but-not-her appearance in some of her films? Taking herself seriously, particularly when required to explain her work, was something that didn't come easily to Akerman. She used humour to deflect the attention. Once, answering questions in Los Angeles, where she had presented *Jeanne Dielman* with the film's lead, Delphine Seyrig, Akerman was asked where she'd found the idea for the film. She replied: 'In a shoe box.' Seyrig reprimanded her afterwards: Akerman had made what most considered a 'masterpiece' but couldn't help undermining it. She had a tendency to do something similar with the inner conflicts which are reflected — albeit sometimes obliquely — in this book. Always ambivalent towards her talent, she begins *Ma mère rit* with: 'I wrote it all down and now I don't like what I've written.'

Ma mère rit was first published in French in 2013 and since then fragments have slowly found their way into English. In the essays, academic articles, and obituaries that appeared around the time of her death in 2015, the book has been used to lay out the underlying intention(s) behind Akerman's films in her own words. Maybe she would have been pleased. *Ma mère rit* has, in a way, given Akerman some posthumous control over those whose concern has long been to find 'answers' in her biography, a tendency that has only intensified since her death. What is it about her? Is it her diversity of styles, her prolific output, or the alleged 'difficulty' of her films? Is it because she often appears in front of the camera, tantalisingly close yet deliberately elusive – both her and not her? Or is it, again, that she existed at the intersection of several marginal identities – as a woman, a lesbian, a Jew and someone of the 'second generation' – with these strands often informing her work? She consistently fought all attempts to align her films with her identity and refused to be shown at film festivals dedicated specifically to women directors, say. But what do those who identify with one or more of these identities do with that? As a queer, Jewish translator, I have heard the voice of my grandmother planning the next evening's meal while translating the voice of Chantal's own mother; and have found it easy to generate a vocabulary for the thinly veiled way in which those around Chantal talk about her queerness.

This translation is one of two to be published within the space of a couple of months on either side of the Atlantic, three years since Akerman's death by suicide. But after suicide, the publication of the last text always carries a risk. For some, it has only intensified the desire to play detective. The book's narrative defies chronology and an easy 'cause and effect' interpretation, yet some think they have found a kind of 'suicide note' towards the end of the text, where Akerman expresses an intention to kill herself after her mother's death. While Akerman evidently enjoyed the freedom from the film industry a book allowed, this grim project seemed the unfortunate but logical conclusion of decades of misogynistic reduction of Akerman's work.

It's perhaps unsurprising, then, that she avoids writing here about her films. The few references to filmmaking in *Ma mère rit* are always made by other people, and illustrate how she was seen as public property: a stranger at a funeral grabs her arm and tells her that she must carry on making films; another says, seemingly out of the blue, that 'it's clear from your films that you put your whole self into them.' Akerman, as a creator, was so much to so many, but many struggled to separate the art from the artist, and to appreciate that she frequently found her role, and the attendant pressures, onerous. Through writing something that would never be adapted for the screen, perhaps she wrested back control. For Akerman, *Ma mère rit* was a piece of work which she didn't regard as work. It was mostly written between meals in a room at the end of the corridor of her mother's apartment. In her short film from 1986, *Portrait d'une paresseuse*, she bemoans the fact that 'to make a film, you have to get up and get dressed.' I like to imagine that she wrote this book in bed, in her pyjamas.

DANIELLA SHREIR
London, July 2019

ILLUSTRATIONS

Photographs from a private collection. Stills produced by LUK Lambrecht for Cultural Center Strombeek.

Films, shorts and installations by Chantal Akerman.

- p. viii-ix: *Histoires d'Amérique: Food, Family and Philosophy* (1989)
- p. 5, 38, 49, 65, 107, 115, 188: *Maniac Shadows* (installation, 2013)
- p. 13: Chantal Akerman and her mother
- p. 15, 23, 83, 149: *Là-bas* (documentary, 2006)
- p. 19: *L'homme à la valise* (1983)
- p. 26: Akerman and her sister
- p. 34, 131, 188: Photographs by Chantal Akerman
- p. 43: Akerman's mother and sister
- p. 52: Akerman, aged one
- p. 56-57: *Jeanne Dielman, 23 quai du Commerce, 1080 Bruxelles* (1975)
- p, 74, 81, 98, 167: *D'Est* (1995)
- p. 91, 123: *La chambre* (1972)
- p. 95, 19: *L'homme à la valise* (1983), photograph by Chantal Akerman
- p. 143: *Portrait d'une jeune fille de la fin des années 60 à Bruxelles* (1994)
- p. 162-163: *Hôtel Monterey* (1972)

Thanks to Marian Goodman.

BY THE SAME AUTHOR

Les Rendez-vous d'Anna, 1977
Hall de nuit, 1991
Un divan à New York, 1996
Une Famille à Bruxelles, 1998
Autoportrait en cinéaste, 2004

FILMOGRAPHY

Saute ma ville, 1968
L'Enfant aimée ou Je joue à être une femme mariée, 1971
La Chambre, 1972
Hôtel Monterey, 1972
Hanging Out Yonkers, 1973
Le 15/8, 1973
Je, tu, il, elle, 1974
Jeanne Dielman, 23, quai du commerce, 1080 Bruxelles, 1975
News from Home, 1977
Les Rendez-vous d'Anna, 1978
Toute une nuit, 1982
Les Années 80, 1983
L'Homme à la valise, 1983
J'ai faim, j'ai froid, 1984
New York, New York bis, 1984
Paris vu par . . . vingt ans après, 1984
Le Marteau, 1986

Letters Home, 1986
Portrait d'une paresseuse (La paresse), 1986
Mallet-Stevens, 1986
Golden Eighties (Window Shopping), 1986
Les Trois Dernières Sonates de Franz Schubert, 1989
Trois strophes sur le nom de Sacher, 1989
Histoires d'Amerique (Food, Family and Philosophy), 1989
Contre l'oubli, 1991
Nuit et Jour, 1991
D'Est, 1993
Portrait d'une jeune fille de la fin des années soixante à Bruxelles, 1994
Un divan à New York, 1996
Sud, 1999
La Captive, 2000
De l'autre côté, 2002
Demain on déménage, 2004
Là-bas, 2006
Women from Antwerp in November, 2008
La Folie Almayer, 2012
No Home Movie, 2015

This book has been selected to receive financial assistance from English PEN's 'PEN Translates' programme, supported by Arts Council England. English PEN exists to promote literature and our understanding of it, to uphold writers' freedoms around the world, to campaign against the persecution and imprisonment of writers for stating their views, and to promote the friendly co-operation of writers and the free exchange of ideas.

www.englishpen.org

First published by Mercure de France, 2013
This edition first published by Silver Press in 2019
silverpress.org

978 0 99571 623 0

Copyright © Estate of Chantal Akerman
Copyright in the foreword © Eileen Myles
Copyright in the introduction © Frances Morgan
All rights reserved

The right of Chantal Akerman to be identified as the
author of this work has been asserted in accordance with
Section 77 of the Copyright, Designs and Patent Act 1988.

4 5 6 7 8 9 10 11 12 13

Design by Rose Nordin
Typeset in Joanna

Printed and bound by CPI Group (UK) Ltd, Croydon, CR0 4YY

All rights reserved. No part of this publication may be
reproduced, stored in a retrieval system or transmitted in
any form or by any means, electronic, mechanical,
photocopying, recording or otherwise, without prior
permission in writing from Silver Press.

EU GPSR Authorised Representative: Logos Europe,
9 rue Nicolas Poussin, 17000, La Rochelle, France.
contact@logoseurope.eu